AMERICAN FOLKLIFE CENTER · THE LIBRARY OF CONGRESS ·

# Folklife

## ANNUAL 1987

*A Publication of the*

AMERICAN FOLKLIFE CENTER

AT THE LIBRARY OF CONGRESS

*Edited by Alan Jabbour and James Hardin*

LIBRARY OF CONGRESS · WASHINGTON · 1988

*From Public Law 94-201, the American Folklife Preservation Act, which created the American Folklife Center in 1976.*

DECLARATION OF FINDINGS AND PURPOSE
*SEC. 2 (a) The Congress hereby finds and declares—*

*(1) that the diversity inherent in American folklife has contributed greatly to the cultural richness of the Nation and has fostered a sense of individuality and identity among the American people;*

*(2) that the history of the United States effectively demonstrates that building a strong nation does not require the sacrifice of cultural differences;*

*(3) that American folklife has a fundamental influence on the desires, beliefs, values, and character of the American people;*

*(4) that it is appropriate and necessary for the Federal Government to support research and scholarship in American folklife in order to contribute to an understanding of the complex problems of the basic desires, beliefs, and values of the American people in both rural and urban areas;*

*(5) that the encouragement and support of American folklife, while primarily a matter for private and local initiative, is also an appropriate matter of concern to the Federal Government; and*

*(6) that it is in the interest of the general welfare of the Nation to preserve, support, revitalize, and disseminate American folklife traditions and arts.*

*(b) It is therefore the purpose of the Act to establish in the Library of Congress an American Folklife Center to preserve and present American folklife.*

*Designed by Adrianne Onderdonk Dudden*

Folklife Annual *presents a yearly collection of articles on the traditional expressive life and culture in America. The articles are written by specialists in folklife and related fields, but the annual is intended for a wide audience. A publication of the American Folklife Center at the Library of Congress,* Folklife Annual *seeks to promote the documentation and study of American folklife, share the traditions, values, and activities of American folk culture, and serve as a national forum for the discussion of ideas and issues in folklore and folklife.*

*The editors will consider for publication articles on all areas of folklife but are particularly interested in the folklife of the United States. Manuscripts should be typewritten, double-spaced, and in accord with the* Chicago Manual of Style. *Submit to: The Editors,* Folklife Annual, *American Folklife Center, Library of Congress, Washington, D.C. 20540.*

*For sale by the Superintendent of Documents, U.S. Government Printing Office, Washington, D.C. 20402*
ISBN 0-8444-0575-2
ISSN 0747-5322

*Cover: Dancer at the Crow Fair in Montana, an annual powwow, August 1979. (MT9-MC27-1) Photograph by Michael S. Crummett*

*Title page: Arlee Powwow, Flathead Reservation, Arlee, Montana, July 5, 1987. (FCP-OS-87-ES-16A-8) Photograph by Edwin Schupman, Jr. American Folklife Center, Library of Congress*

# Contents

# Preface

A phrase in Roger Abrahams's article on the Afro-American folktale provides a unifying theme for the 1987 volume of *Folklife Annual:* "strategies for survival in a hostile world." Abrahams shows that folktales contain hidden cultural meanings that go beyond these strategies, that they are more than guarded parables of life under slavery in the United States (as some critics have thought). But he also shows that they *are* strategies in a larger sense, affirmations of vitality, models of "how to get and keep things going even in the face of death."

Such a strategy informs Erika Brady's essay on the beau geste, a literary concept Brady invokes to account for certain kinds of private acts. She brings the folklorist's sense of the importance of ritual to her interpretation of behavior she observed in those suffering from the death of a friend or relative. And in an odd way, the apparent futility and bravado of the character in the Old John story Abrahams mentions, flying wildly about the Heaven from which he is about to be ousted, a "flying piece of furniture," parallel the desperate need for symbolic action felt by so many Brady encountered: when death has stripped life of meaningful action, some deep impulse allows, even demands, action of any sort. Even an action invented by an individual may have the effect of reawakening the power of symbols to infuse life with meaning.

The American Indian powwow has flourished in the face of another threat of extinction, that suffered by Native Americans and their culture as the European settler moved across the American continent. Impressions of the powwow in the western and northern Plains are chronicled by Vanessa Brown, a participant, and Barre Toelken, a folklorist who has studied Native American culture for many years. The photographs that ac-

company the article were selected from the Library of Congress collections in the Prints and Photographs Division and the American Folklife Center and show powwows on the Crow Reservation in Montana and the Omaha Reservation in Macy, Nebraska.

Despite the evolution of Native American gatherings, there are similarities in the dance and costume depicted in these photographs and the images captured in the paintings of artists George Catlin and Carl Bodmer in the nineteenth century. James Gilreath of the Library's Rare Book and Special Collections Division describes the making of these paintings and the publication of the books that have preserved them for us. The bringing together of thirties photographs from the Library's Farm Security Administration Collection, recent ones from the Center, and the earlier images by Bodmer and Catlin from the Rare Book and Special Collections Division is intentional and demonstrates one of the many possibilities for folklife research at the Library of Congress.

The powwow has become a principal means of maintaining certain elements of a continuing Indian culture (both tribal and pan-Indian), while providing a context for passing traditional ways along to young people. Sam Cronk, Beverley Cavanagh, and Franziska von Rosen offer an anatomy of such events in Canada's northeastern provinces, showing their energy and variety. Originating in the Great Plains, the powwow has now spread to most of the states in this country and to many of the Canadian provinces.

Traditional culture is important to the many ethnic schools established throughout the country, where language study is the principal enterprise and ethnic identity the principal purpose. The very fact of the schools may be a surprise: that there are so many and that they exist in such variety. The American Folklife Center launched a study of these schools in 1982, and excerpts from four reports from the study are presented here. Longer versions of these reports along with ten others are available from the Center as *Ethnic Heritage and Language Schools in America*. Taken together the reports offer evidence of a nation far more culturally diverse than may be supposed, yet with common threads in the strategies employed by various cultures to maintain ethnic identity in the American context.

The language of the black community has found expression in the folktale and the sermon, and the two forms reveal interesting contrasts within the life of the community. African and Afro-American folktales contain elements that are at odds with conventional morality, but a moral element is highly evident in the black sermon, presented here by Jeff Todd Titon in his account of the life and career of the Reverend C. L. Franklin. In the particular form of the chanted sermon, however, there is something deeper than moral dictum, something that speaks through poetry to the life of the people in the congregation.

John Henry Faulk was one of the first in the white community to acknowledge the beauty and importance of the black ser-

mon. In an interview conducted by James McNutt, Faulk relates his early experiences, the attitudes he encountered, and his work with some of the pioneers of folklore studies. Through study of the sermons and songs collected in the thirties and forties from black and Hispanic peoples, Faulk and others were able to penetrate social and cultural stereotypes.

This poetry and music came to be intimately connected with the civil rights movement in the sixties, so that early strategies for survival became strategies for change in a society that denied opportunities on the basis of difference. Increasingly, what Faulk calls our "solid understanding of what this republic is all about" must accommodate itself to the fact of our national cultural diversity, from the descendants of the earliest native peoples to the most recently arrived from Cambodia or El Salvador.

JH

# Eating in the Belly of the Elephant

## BY ROGER D. ABRAHAMS

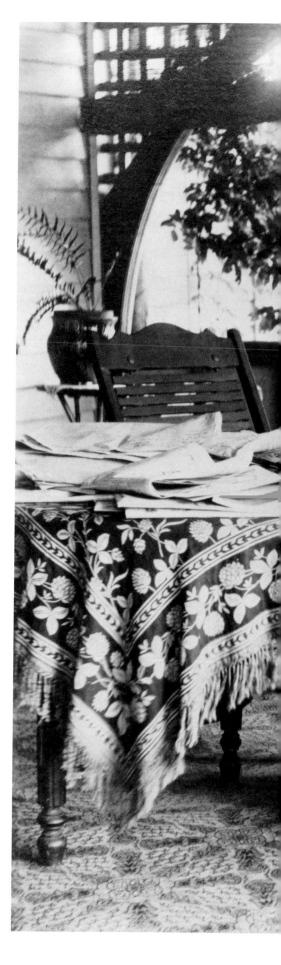

The belly of an elephant seems an unlikely place from which to launch a folktale. But it is in just such extraordinary places that we often discover the protagonist of Afro-American tales. Every culture develops its own secret places in which the narrative imagination is given free rein and artful lying is encouraged. And the difference of these worlds is dramatized for Western readers whenever they encounter folktales from the oral storytellers of other cultures. This is hardly surprising. But because of the popularity of the books of Joel Chandler Harris, Afro-American stories have become as familiar as those we inherited from Europe. The Uncle Remus stories have been domesticated, in fact, made a part of the common reader's notion of what a folktale is by virtue of Harris's ability to give them such a strong personal voice and to set them out as if they were capricious adventures that have a strong sense of beginning and ending.

However, folktales are told throughout

*Joel Chandler Harris at his home, "Wren's Nest," 1900. Prints and Photographs Division, Library of Congress*

Copyright © 1988 Roger D. Abrahams

the black world—on both sides of the Atlantic—with no such sense of wholeness in their actual telling. Everyone knows these stories, and everyone listening is expected to enter into the performance of their telling. At those times at night when tales are appropriately told, someone may begin by singing a song identified with the story or by having someone shout out one of its recurrent lines. They may be launched with a formula like "Once upon a time and a very long time" and finished off by a phrase equally indefinite—such as "The pin bend, and right there my story end"—but this is far from the only way. And the idea that one person tells the story while all of the others listen is not the most common, unless the stories are directed by an adult to a group of children. In the usual community performance, the voice of the storyteller is far from the only one heard. Comments, exclamations, criticisms, repetitions of the most dramatic lines merge in the welter of sound that constitutes the tale's telling. Most tales have songs arising out of the action of the story, and the audience joins in at such points, often taking the telling of the tale away from the one who initiated it, not only by repeating the song again and again but by getting up and dancing to the music as well.

Even when they are excerpted from this communal setting, the "texts" of stories from the black world exist in an imaginative world as different from the Western fairy tale as those from "The Arabian Nights" and any other of the world's make-believe traditions. The European tradition of fairy tales prepares us primarily for the success-stories of Jack, Cinderella, and the Frog-Prince, all unfulfilled characters who find dramatic ways of revealing their true, beautiful, and powerful selves through a stolen kiss, a touch, even a successfully purloined goose. In contrast, black tales, especially those carried on in the New World, commonly revolve around the outrageous contrivances of Trickster: Br'er Rabbit in the United States and the Bahamas, Compé Anansi, the spider, in most of the rest of the hemisphere. Far from being magical renderings of success stories, in which the world is made whole through the "happily ever after" final action, Afro-American stories commonly end with some statement of the frailty of friendship and the scattering of the community: "And that's why Lion lives in the bush, and Rabbit in town" or something of that sort. Such stories rely for their comic effect on the fact that they are being told from within a group that is proclaiming its own sense of togetherness by the very telling and singing and dancing of the story.

Even in their most familiar literary renderings, as given us by J. C. Harris or Walt Disney, these stories are full of actions that are capricious and motivated by greed. These tales carry the listener into strange worlds, indeed. For Br'er Rabbit and the other Afro-American figures of Trickster live in the nooks and crannies, on the frontier between the human and animal worlds. From such a vantage, they are able to act as if no place is out of bounds. By seizing this license, Trickster ventures brazenly into the secret places of the natural or the social world: on the one hand, he sneaks into the depths of "the bush"; on the other, he devises ways to enter the king's private realm, his yard, his palace, even into the bedroom of his beautiful daughter. In these forbidden and mysterious places, encounters take place that detail deceptions, reveal mysteries, and usually end with a feeling that the manic acts of Trickster tear apart the fabric of life even in this imaginary world.

These stories, like European fairy tales, have been subjected to a good deal of psychological and sociological perusal, most of it centering on the stories' ability to provide strategies for survival in a hostile world. The most common European-style fairy tales do, indeed, describe the efforts of the young to find a way out of their particular family situations. These success stories illustrate a way for those with little power to escape from their lowly status: find an outside resource, get help from someone outside the family and community, and a personal and social transformation will occur. The hero is often the child who is lowest in the pecking order, either because of age or, in the case of heroine, a step-daughter status.

The success pattern of such tales is seen to reflect the historical struggle for social, cultural, or psychological autonomy, making them central documents in the achievement of modernity. That such upward mobility and reversal of the social order differ from our usual vision of a *folk*—that is, a peasant—strategy becomes clear when seen in this way, pace Bruno Bettelheim in his *Uses of Enchantment*. To regard folk tales of any sort as models for behavior (or even attitude) without understanding the range of behaviors available to those telling and listening to the tales is to ask for misunderstanding of how these stories have been maintained and used. It seems misleading, then, to approach tales primarily in terms of providing patterns of individuation in communities that might not value such an individualistic approach to life.

Folktales from the black world have also been approached from such a perspective, but with even less revealing results. Trickster's wiliness and voraciousness represent the only available strategies for success for those living under slavery or in its aftermath. This is wrongheaded in a number of ways. Most of the same stories are told in Africa, and under very different social and cultural conditions, and therefore can hardly be regarded as arising from the conditions of slavery—though they certainly are employed to comment on servility and its alternatives. Additionally, the pattern of the stories can hardly be regarded as embodying success, for Trickster is not able to bring about any change of status for himself. He merely satisfies his hungers while exercising his wits. The only changes he is able to accomplish, in fact, are to bring everyone around him down to his own level, so that he may laugh at them, even kill or eat them. In one story, for instance, Spider tricks Whale and Elephant into having a tug-of-war without their knowing who they are actually pulling against. In Harris's rendering of the story, Rabbit gets two stronger animals to pull a rope tied to a tree!

In another called "The Signifying Monkey," common in the repertoire of American rhyming *toast*-tellers, Monkey convinces Lion that Elephant has been saying bad things about him, thus engineering an epic battle that Monkey witnesses from a tree. Unfortunately, he gets too excited about what he has been able to bring about, slips and falls, and is caught by the enraged Lion, already badly beaten by the Elephant. These are not success stories; the audience obviously delights in them because of the situations the animals, large and small, get themselves into.

Yet it is widely thought that the trickster tales embody the only available strategies for survival under conditions in which the taletellers and their audience have no control over their own lives. While he hardly originated the theory, Joel Chandler Harris pursues this line of thought in the introduction to his first collection, *Uncle Remus: His Songs and His Sayings:* "it needs no scientific investigation to show why [the Negro] selects as his hero the weakest and most harmless of all animals, and brings him out victorious in contests with the bear, the wolf and the fox. It is not virtue that triumphs but helplessness." What he does not bother to notice is that Rabbit dreams up and stage-manages most of these confrontations.

Harris was explicitly involved in using these stories as a way of building an image of the New South after the Civil War. He found these stories a useful way of dramatizing the warm relationships that arose on the plantation between young children and old house-slaves. Later in his introduction, Harris argues that Br'er Rabbit does not act out of malice but out of mischievousness, thus underscoring the idea that plantation blacks took as their model this childlike character. But the stories themselves belie his point, for there is much crass selfishness in Rabbit's actions, and he is able to engineer incredible acts of violence, ones which Uncle Remus himself has to account for in some strange ways.

Harris, himself, was worried that the tales would be misconstrued in a different way. "I am advised by my publishers that

*Brer Rabbit. Illustration by A. B. Frost from* Uncle Remus: His Songs and His Sayings

this book will be included in their catalogue of humorous publications. . . . however humorous it may be in effect, its intention is perfectly serious." And this intention was to demonstrate that there were authentic traditions that had been carried on by the slave, lore brought into plantation life from Africa. He was confronting a public that identified anything written in dialect with the comic routines of the blackface minstrel performer. Nevertheless, his papers reveal that he had embarked on a truly serious endeavor: to bring to public attention authentic traditions of Afro-Americans in the face of the fakelore being contrived for them in the "cake walks," the "coon songs," and the other types of performance carried out in blackface on the minstrel stage.

Harris's aims were manifest: to dramatize the humane dimension of the plantation system by depicting the ongoing affectionate relationship between the old retainer, Uncle Remus, and "the boy." But, in the process of developing this picture, he discovered a desire to put into the mouth of Uncle Remus and his other storytelling characters only authentic songs, sayings, and stories that he heard himself or that other whites sent to him from their remembrances of life on the plantation. He became not only a confirmed student of black language, effectively developing a literary style of transcription that caught the nuances of the different dialects in his area of the Old South, but he also became an avid collector of tales. He collected by having discussions on the subject and by engaging in correspondence with other whites who had had similar experiences with family retainers who had raised them. Consequently, the tales he discovered were those stories black performers found suitable to tell to white children, and told in a style appropriate to the audience as well. But, given these limitations, the material he presents is, in fact, characteristic of the stories still told in many Afro-American village communities throughout the New World.

By telling of the ways in which he first encountered and later collected this material, he impressed upon his contemporary readers that they were being led into a previously hidden magical kingdom. By this, he not only made others aware of this rich vein of stories in our midst but also encouraged further collections. Moreover, he created a popular audience for the stories, not only in the United States but throughout the world. Indeed, in the last half of the nineteenth century (and well into the twentieth century) Americans abroad found themselves being called upon to perform in black style of song and dance, because of the popularity of the minstrel show, or to tell Uncle Remus stories: Mark Twain himself built upon such expectations and flavored his performances with such tales, crediting them to the powerful art of his friend Joel Chandler Harris.

This newfound interest in Br'er Rabbit stories led to a flurry of collecting and pub-

lishing of Afro-American traditional stories. Harris was highly regarded for his work by the leaders of the New England literary establishment. He was not only enrolled as a founding member of the American Folklore Society, being started in Cambridge by members of the group surrounding James Russell Lowell and Francis James Child, but the first issues of the *Journal of American Folklore* in the late 1880s contained a number of stories from Afro-American sources and commentary on the African ancestry of this body of material.

One of the first local chapters of the folklore organization was started at Hampton Institute, and a number of the teachers there, black and white, collected and published lore from students, including some of their animal stories. And Franz Boas, the leading figure in the society in the first quarter of this century, encouraged Afro-

American literary figures such as Arthur Huff Fauset and Zora Neale Hurston to make field trips to black communities. For Hurston, this resulted in a return to her home in Florida in the 1920s to collect songs and stories from her neighbors, a project which led to the writing of her masterpiece, *Mules and Men*.

As Hurston and other Afro-Americans began to record their own traditions, it became clear that there were many stories and styles of performance that were unknown to whites. Her book departs radically from previous collections in bringing out the group hilarity and involvement in the actual telling of the tales, and in the stories she reports featuring an open, if comic, conflict between blacks and whites. These protest stories seemed to confirm the idea that Afro-Americans not only had many benign public forms of entertainment that they performed in the presence of outsiders but also a body of hidden lore. These stories remind us that mystery remains a powerful resource in face-to-face relations, especially when there is a disparity of power between those who are interacting.

One story, common in Afro-America, makes this point dramatically: John, the prototypical clever slave, is out in a field one day and bumps into a skull that talks to him, much to his amazement. He runs to his master, telling him of this wonder, and, of course, the master doesn't believe John's story. John finally persuades him to come at least to see the skull. When they get to it, John tries to enter into the discussion again, but the skull speaks not, and John gets a whipping for his troubles. When Old Master leaves, John asks the skull why it didn't say anything, and it responds: "Haven't you learned not to open your big trap to the white man yet?"

On its very surface, this story is a parable about how to act (and how not to act) in front of whites. But it carries larger messages as well, for it has been collected with a great many other "keep your business to yourself" punchlines that are directed not toward whites at all but toward the gossipers within the black community. Perhaps of greater significance, this story has been collected throughout Africa, where it carries the same general message of how important it is to maintain control over one's own words.

There are many black stories constructed in much this same way: situation comedies that elicit laughter because a character has foolishly put himself on the spot. Some of these are elaborated, on occasion, into stories in which blacks and whites confront each other, but many others aren't. And sometimes, the very same story may find its way into the repertoire of storytellers on both sides of the color line. For instance, one of the staple situations in black joking sessions, as in white ones, concerns the problems that occur at the Heavenly Gates when a recently dead man confronts St. Peter with his power and his rules. In black jokes, the applicant is often referred to simply as "this colored man" or some other generic label, and is turned away simply because of his color. In one story, he manages to sneak in but doesn't know how to put on his wings and manages to botch the job. He flies around in such an eccentric way and knocks so many things over that his presence comes to St. Peter's notice, and he is thrown out of the place without any ceremony. As he leaves, he says: "Well, I may not have been in heaven long, but I was a flying piece of furniture while I was there."

This is a story in which race and clownishness seem to be equated. It has been reported from white performers, where it makes fun of the obvious sneakiness and clumsiness of the applicant at the Gates. But, of course, this is hardly how the joke is interpreted when told among blacks. Here one encounters a note of admiration for this poor old guy who is able to seize the moment and make the most of it—especially in the face of the old time "Whites Only" sign at the Heavenly Portals.

These jokes, with the more elaborate folktales, place a high value on the ability to act, to improvise as possibilities arise, even when the whole thing may blow up in the face of the adventurer. This is precisely the attraction of Trickster, of course: his brazen willingness to try anything if it promises to stir things up. In fact, in much of Afro-America, all jokes, since they involve this kind of foolishness or nonsense, are regarded as the property of Trickster and are told in his name, as "Anansi Stories" or "Buh Rabbit stuff," whether or not one or the other is actually one of the characters.

*The Talking Skull. Illustration by Joshua Tolford for* Congo Fireside Tales *by Phyllis Savory (New York: Hastings House Publishers Limited, 1962). Reprinted with permission*

Cinderella Ties on the Slipper.

*"Cinderella Tries on the Slipper." Frontispiece from* Cinderella and the Glass Slipper *(Boston: Lothrop Publishing Company, 1899)*

As tales that tell of nonsensical and outrageous behavior in the name of Trickster, they may be too strong, too coarse for those readers coming to them expecting stories about the strivings of Cinderella and Prince Charming. Consider the story to which I alluded at the very beginning: the adventures of Trickster going into the belly of the elephant and gorging himself by feeding on the innards he finds there. Like the more familiar "Ali Baba and the Forty Thieves," a protagonist discovers a cache of riches only to get caught there because of his greediness. In the story of entering the elephant's belly, Trickster hears from a friend that there are some huge elephants down in the King's corral. Always on the prowl for new adventures, Trickster is immediately interested. The friend warns the outrageous Trickster that he must restrain himself, for if he overindulges the elephant will die, and if he is still inside, he will be trapped by the King's guard. So his friend shows him where to hide until the guard is looking elsewhere, and how to sneak into the elephant yard, pick out a big one, crawl up through the anus and intestines into the belly, and there he will find all the food he might want. Trickster follows these instructions and finds himself there in the belly of the elephant. He becomes so excited on seeing all of this food, that he cuts away with abandon, cramming food into his mouth as quickly as he can. Ignoring the friend's warning, in his willful and impulsive way, he takes one slice too many and the elephant collapses. Trapped, he begins yelling; the elephant keeper comes over to see what all the noise is about, and he is caught.

This story is interesting in its similarities to and differences from the more familiar fairy tales, like "Little Red Riding Hood," which find the hero or heroine in the belly of a beast and in need of rescue. In the fairy tales, this predicament arises because the protagonist is pursued by the hungry and conniving animal; in the Afro-American tale, Trickster willfully sneaks into these private places and finds himself trapped there. While many of the fairy tales involve explorations of forbidden territory, they are utilitarian adventures, seeking an object or formula that will give them goods or capabilities useful to them in the "real" world. This power gives the hero a new status on his return. And where there are heroes of this stripe, there will be villains as well, ogre figures who may be killed legitimately. But poor elephant is simply a food resource, and his death is neither to be mourned nor cheered.

It is at these very points that the folktale terrain looks strangest, and our Euro-American ability to find our way around becomes severely tested. Euro-American stories tend to focus on the deeds of a single protagonist as he makes his way to the secret of knowledge. African and Afro-American tales also focus on a protagonist finding his way into secret places. But discovering the source of mystery cannot be translated to human uses. Rather, the protagonist who makes the discovery finds it necessary to keep the new resource to himself. In black stories, in other words, the bush and the village are two different worlds that can only coexist in dramatic opposition. While fairy tales have heroes who come from the bosom of a family and the heart of a community, black folktales feature a figure who is neither of one world or the other; rather, like spider or rabbit, he lives on the margins between the two worlds with access to both but with power in neither except to reveal the mysteries of nature or humanity that he has been able to observe.

Like the story of the conversation with the skull, as well as the one about sneaking into the elephant's belly, a good portion of the repertoire of black tales came to the New World with the slaves, representing one of the many ways in which African traditions have been adapted to changing cultural circumstances. But the carryover is much greater than simply a matter of repertoire. The point missed by those who have read the Br'er Rabbit stories as entertainments featuring a protagonist who is simply mischievous is that they are told in serious times, such as at wakes, when they are employed as ways of celebrating community even while the basic values of community life, and especially acting responsibly and respectably, are being tested. Trickster, in such a case, represents a kind of wild-eyed confirmation of the importance of vitality and inventiveness. But the stories are not (*pace* Harris) about a harmless scamp; they are concerned with out-and-out malicious nonsense, about rude and often violently indecent action, carried out by characters who are only fit to live in the nooks and crannies, in the rafters or under the bed, and who do things that are only worthy of being laughed at.

In essence, the direction and meaning of stories differ considerably in the two great traditions, even in those cases where something like the same story is part of the repertoire. An example: both traditions have many stories that focus on a transformation of character through a change of clothing. Cinderella, for instance, is such a story, for the heroine is introduced, among other ways, through the terrible condition of her clothes. Slowly but dramatically, her rags-and-tatters getup is replaced by clothing fit for a princess; and, as we (and Prince Charming) come to realize, the wardrobe makes the woman. Cinderella's elevation in life is symbolized by what she comes to wear on her back and feet. Now compare this to that most common of African tales, that of the animal-courter, which Amos Tutuola uses as the central fable of his *The Palm-Wine Drunkard*. In this tale a man comes to court the chief's beautiful daughter; he is handsome beyond description, and he comes out the victor in the contest for her hand or, at least, for her favors. The time comes for them to leave to go to his home-village and they set off merrily; but as they go into the bush, he sheds first one piece of clothing, then another, one limb and then another, until he is shown to be a beast (usually a snake) in disguise. He has borrowed these human attributes and now he must give them back.

In a widely found Afro-American rendering of this story there are further complications. The king's beautiful daughter is wooed away by an animal in human form. He also has a son, the Old Witch Boy, an outcast who lives under the bed or in the ash heap and sneaks around the yard spying on everybody. As he has witching powers, he is able to recognize the character of his sister's suitor, but when he tries to warn their father, no one listens. He stealthily follows his sister and her lover into the bush and discovers the magical formula the animal uses to take on his human disguise. The boy returns and is now able to convince his father. They go to the bush, the boy sings the magical song, the animal returns to his natural form, and Massa King kills him. In none of these cases is the transformed creature permitted to remain in the world to which he or she does not belong. Moreover, the poor Old Witch Boy seems to gain nothing but a little attention through his unmasking move.

Solving the mystery not only does not alter the power-structure of the "royal family"; it seems to intensify the outsider status of the Old Witch Boy. Like Trickster, he knows the secrets of both the home and the bush but can only scamper back and forth between them. He has the power to break things apart, but not to bring any kind of social order out of the encounter. Just as discovering the way into the elephant's belly means getting caught there, discovering the bad situation his sister has gotten into wins him little love once he gets home.

Not all African story forms weathered the transatlantic crossing. Especially notable in their absence are the moral tales and heroic epics still found widely in sub-saharan Africa. This is not to say there are no traditional forms of performance in Afro-America that discuss the right and wrong ways to act. But such moral vigilance is no longer contained within the story traditions as it is in Africa. Rather, moral messages are maintained in the oratorical and sermon traditions of the black preacher and community leader, those who preside over the most serious occasions of the community. Storytelling, in the main, on this side of the Atlantic has been relegated to the status of entertainments, lies, nonsense. And in that part of the black world in which the great nonsense occasion is the nine-night wake, tales become words put into actions that discuss the very notion of vitality. It is almost as if the unstated so-

*Bra Spider in the African Village. Illustration by Christine Price from* Singing Tales of Africa, *retold by Adjai Robinson (New York: Charles Scribner's Sons, 1974). Copyright © 1974 Christine Price. Reprinted by permission*

cial premise of such communities is that the real subject of the tales is how to get and keep things going even in the face of death.

One might derive some pan-human upbeat message from the tales that have been preserved from the African past: stories which have been read as the testimony of a people who have endured with humor, even if it is of the barbed sort. But what does this do to those who are credited with such endurance? It maintains Afro-Americans and their culture in the same position in relation to "mainstream" culture as they have had for two hundred years: as a resource for new forms and new artistic styles. This continues to place the storyteller alongside the bluesman as a commentator on the strange things that life brings us. This is simply one more stereotype, arising from the alienated segment of the middle class constantly on the lookout for "types" who give forth equally disengaged interpretations of life. But how much help does this provide for those who still have to scuffle for a living, even if they no longer have to shuffle quite so much.

More important is the widespread recognition that there are, indeed, a hidden culture and a mysterious lore that have been maintained within Afro-American communities. But its secrets are not ones, in the main, which have been self-consciously concealed. No, they have been kept within a community and carried out in situations that anyone who does not come from this culture will find difficult to understand. Joel Chandler Harris introduced some of these characters and the most palatable of the stories to American readers. But that introduction took place over a hundred years ago and reflects an earlier style of flirtation with the inventory of black performance. Surely, after all of this time and after other deep black forms have become a part of the American repertoire of popular styles, we are at the point where we ought to acknowledge that an Afro-American culture has been maintained despite the forces that assume the assimilation or the elimination of alternative ways of performing and creating. Such an acknowledgment would be the first step in understanding the systematic character as well as the vigor and integrity of the culture.

# Crawling into the Elephant's Belly

One time, all the animals were looking around for food, but there was none to be had. Anansi and his family were starving too, and he didn't know what he could do about it. One day, he saw this old elephant come out of the king's park and he got an idea. That night, he climbed the wall to the palace where all the elephants were kept. He crept up to one of them while it was asleep and went in there behind his tail and crawled way up into his belly. And when he got there he just chopped off a little piece of meat, and he sneaked back out and carried the meat home.

Anansi went back night after night, crawling into the belly of one of the elephants, and each morning, just before daybreak, he sneaked back home.

Now, Anansi's friend Yawarri the Anteater saw that Anansi was getting fat and here he was as hungry as ever. He tried to get Anansi to tell him where he was getting his food every morning; but Anansi put him off the scent by telling him one lie after another.

Yawarri was so hungry that he got sick too. He told his friend Monkey about how he felt and how hard it was to watch Anansi growing fat while he and his family were starving. When Monkey heard all this, he told Yawarri to keep a watch near Anansi's house at night, and to follow him to see where he was going to get his food. Yawarri took this advice. He watched Anansi's house, and when Anansi came out he followed his footsteps until they got to the king's palace. Anansi didn't know Yawarri was there. He went to climb the wall of the king's park; then Yawarri called out to him and told him that if he didn't promise to take him in as a partner he would yell out that someone was sneaking into the king's yard and stealing things.

So Anansi promised, and took Yawarri with him that night. Anansi told him how he did this every night. While the king's elephants slept in the park, he went through the asshole and into the stomach of one of them, cut off a small piece of meat, and came back out without waking the elephants. And he made sure that he never tried this trick on the same elephant, so that none of them would ever know what he was doing.

When Anansi and Yawarri had gone into the yard a little way, they came up to two elephants, and each went into the bowels of one of them. Anansi, after cutting his usual little piece of meat, came out of his elephant. But Yawarri was a selfish kind of animal, anyhow, and he had been hungry for such a long time that he stayed in there eating a long time. Anansi waited a long time for him, and finally yelled out: "Bru Yawarri! Bru Yawarri! Come out, or the day will soon be here!" Yawarri put his head out, and told Anansi: "Oh, Bru! What fat meat there is in here! I can't come out yet. You go on and send back my wife and children to help me take home what I cut." So Yawarri stayed in there, eating and eating until he was full—and just then the elephant dropped over dead because Yawarri had eaten so much of his belly.

Now, the king was vexed, seeing that one of his best elephants was dead. So he ordered the belly split open to see why he had died. The elephant keepers came back and told the king that when they cut inside the elephant's belly they heard this strange noise. The king sent them back to find out what was making this noise, and there they found Yawarri, still cutting off pieces of meat and eating them.

Now the king was really angry. He told his men to kill Yawarri and to keep a better watch from now on. Now, Anansi had carried the message to Yawarri's wife and children, and they got excited, since they were very hungry too. When they climbed over the wall that night, the elephant keepers were there waiting and shot the whole family.

So that's what comes of being too greedy.
—*Guyana*

# A Flying Fool

This colored man died and went up there to meet his Maker. But when he got to the gates, St. Peter said that God wasn't home or having any visitors—by which he meant no negroes allowed. Well, this old boy, he had been a good man all his life and his preacher had told him that Heaven would be his place, so he didn't exactly know what to do. So he just kind of hung around the gates, until one time St. Peter just had to go and take a pee. So while Pete was gone, this old boy slipped through, stole himself a pair of wings, and he really took off. Sailed around the trees, in and out of those golden houses and all, swooped down and buzzed some of those heavenly singers and all, and had himself a good old time. Meanwhile, of course, St. Pete came back and found out what had happened and called out the heavenly police force to go get him. Well, this guy was just getting the feel of wearing wings, and he really took off, zoomed off. They had some little time bringing him down, him flying all over Heaven fast as he could go. Finally, they got him cornered and he racked up on one of those trees, and I tell you, he looked like a mess with broken wings and all. So they took him and threw him out the gates. Now here comes one of his friends, who asked him, "What happened, man?" He said, "Oh, man, when I got here they wouldn't let me in to the white man's Heaven, but I grabbed me some wings and I had me a fly." He said, "Oh yeah?" Man said, "Yeah, they may not let any colored folks in, but while I was there I was a flying fool."

—*Texas*

Reprinted from *Afro-American Folktales*, ed. Roger D. Abrahams (New York: Pantheon Books, a Division of Random House, Inc., 1985). Copyright © 1985 Roger D. Abrahams

# The "Beau Geste"

## Shaping Private Rituals of Grief

BY ERIKA BRADY

W hen Paulinus of York arrived in Northumbria as a Christian missionary in A.D. 627, King Edwin called a council of his chief advisers to weigh the merits of the new religion. In the course of the discussion, one of the councillors recalled having seen a sparrow blunder through a door into the dining hall in winter. The little bird came in from the darkness and storms of rain and snow outside, flew around for a bit in the firelight, then blundered out once more into the cold night. This, remarked the councillor, is the story of the lives of all men: "of what went before, or what is to follow, we are utterly ignorant." The council adopted the new religion that at last offered some assurance concerning the before and after.[1]

The mystery that precedes and concludes human life has inspired responses of great richness and variety. Deaths among our family and friends leave us heavy with what

we wish we had told them and what remains to be said. Expressions as impersonal as Brezhnev's state funeral, as impressive as the Taj Mahal, and as highly wrought as the Mozart Requiem all testify to a human need to act in response to the fact of death.

Research by folklorists into the traditions associated with death has concentrated on the analytic description of communal ritual and practice, leaving the study of private behavior of the bereaved to psychologists and thanatologists. Nevertheless, I have found academic and field experience in folklore a valuable resource in working with patients and families in a Washington, D.C., hospice and a midwestern hospital's pastoral care program. In particular, my attention has been drawn to certain actions I call examples of the "beau geste."

The name is drawn from the novel of that title published by Percival Christopher Wren. In the book, the hero Michael Geste is nicknamed "Beau" for his dashing appearance. Given to grandly romantic gestures, as a boy he institutes a mock "Viking funeral" to mark great occasions, burning a tin soldier afloat on a toy boat heaped with "treasures."

Later in the novel, an impetuous attempt to save the honor of a loved aunt who has stolen a family necklace lands the brothers in the French Foreign Legion, and Beau is murdered in a mutiny at notorious Fort Zinderneuf.

In a dramatic climax, Beau's twin brother gives him an improvised Viking funeral.

"I pulled myself together, crawled over to where Beau lay, heaved him up in my arms, and carried him below to his own bed in the barrack-room. All round his cot I laid piles of wood from the cook-house and drenched it with lamp oil. I did my best to make it a real 'Viking's Funeral' for him, just like we used to have at home. Just like he used to want it. My chief regret was that I had no Union Jack to drape over him."[2]

The "Beau Geste" of the title comes to represent not only the hero's name, but also the superbly gallant deeds of Beau and his brothers, first in shielding their aunt and later by the symbolic gesture of the "Viking's funeral."

*"Rosa Centifolia," from P. J. Redouté,* Choix des Plus Belle Fleurs *(Rosenwald no. 1910), vol. 2. Rare Book and Special Collections Division*

*Rosa Centifolia*       *Rosier à cent feuilles.*

P. J. Redouté       Langlois

Such actions are not only found in the pages of adventure fiction. Hospital patients and members of their families have told me of their own symbolic enactments and expressions of grief. Perhaps less showy than a Viking funeral or Saharan holocaust, their beau gestes are nonetheless eloquent expressions of love and defiance in the face of confusion and loss.

Characteristically, the beau geste is a mourner's reverent and symbolically charged disposal of an item or items associated with the dead, or a personally composed ritual enacted in his or her memory. By its very nature, the "beau geste" is a private rather than communal statement. Burial with religious items such as rosaries, medals, Bibles, and crosses is common, but as it often represents a denominationally or communally endorsed practice rather than one recalling a quality, inclination, or habit of the deceased, such an inclusion does not represent a beau geste in the strict sense. In contrast to conventional burial inclusions, the beau geste is not only highly personal but often purposely unconventional, even *anti*-conventional. I have been told of burials that included in the casket such diverse and idiosyncratic items as a six-pack of beer, several miniature bottles of Jack Daniels whiskey, a harmonica, a favorite pipe, and keys and wallet still containing the deceased's driver's license and charge cards. Syndicated columnist Mike Royko described and verified an Illinois woman's burial in a Chicago Cubs sweater, with a 1987 Cubs schedule by her side in the casket.[3] My own great-grandfather, a Dane from the Virgin Islands, was buried with his horse and hounds, who were put down at the time of his death to accompany him.

The beau geste is most frequently found in instances where the death results in the highest level of emotional trauma for the bereaved. Considered by professional therapists to be the most irreparable loss an individual can sustain, the grief brought about by the death of a child often finds a limited expression if not solace in personalized symbolic gestures in the form of burial inclusions, specially composed graveside rit-

uals, and other similar actions. So well recognized is this form of expression, that it is common in the case of the death of a child for the funeral director to ask if the parents wish the child to be buried with a favorite toy or book, in a kind of institutionalization of the beau geste. Elisabeth Kübler-Ross, in clinical work with families of dying children, has observed that the siblings of a child dead after long illness, in paying a final visit to the body of their brother or sister, will often spontaneously bring a letter, flower, or toy to slip into the casket under the pillow—a practice which she strongly encourages.[4] Burial with such loved items in these instances seems to offer comfort not only by allowing the giver to send a part of himself or herself along with the dead but also by assuaging the terrible irrational fear common to parents and siblings that the child will be lonely, feel abandoned in death, or miss the special blanket or bear that was a comfort in life.

Next to loss of a child, loss of a spouse represents a grief that conventional expressions of mourning often fail to satisfy. Consequently, the survivor often turns to private and personal means of expression of grief in composing a beau geste. A farmer's wife told me of placing her husband's transistor radio, battered from having been carried about with him on his chores, in the casket with him—even making sure it had fresh batteries. In a well-known nineteenth-century episode, the artist and poet Dante Gabriel Rossetti buried a book that constituted the sole copy of a number of his poems with his wife, Elizabeth, only to find it necessary some years later to have her body exhumed in order to retrieve the book's contents.[5]

The loss of a loved one is particularly difficult for those whose relationship with the deceased was socially ambiguous, giving them no clearly recognized social role in communal rituals surrounding a death. A twentieth-century episode recounted to me echoes the Rossetti tragedy, with a contemporary twist. Corinne D., a sophisticated

Washingtonian, had been involved with a married man separated from his wife. He was an alcoholic, and Corinne had refused to see him again until he sought professional help for his drinking. He had threatened suicide on a number of occasions, but she had ceased taking his threats seriously—until, after a frantic phone call in which he as before reported that he was going to take an overdose of sleeping pills, she did not hear from him for several days. She found him dead in his apartment. The pieces of a bone ring she had given him lay next to his hand, having split off his finger as the body swelled. After taking up the pieces, she called the police. From that point, the funeral arrangements were in the hands of her lover's estranged wife, leaving Corinne with no defined role to play aside from that of the many mourners who were not members of the immediate family. Privately, she begged the funeral director to place the pieces of the broken ring in the casket with her lover.

In a similar episode reported to me, also in Washington, Sean H. lost his lover to AIDS. Although the dead man's family had had little to do with him for some years, for the purposes of burial they represented the next of kin. Sean slit the heel off one of the shoes that he was to take with other clothing to the funeral home for the burial, and cut a hollow large enough to conceal a small lucky charm that had been a gift from him to his dead friend.

When the beau geste is performed within a few days of a death, it tends to be in the form of a burial inclusion or disposal of some object at or near the gravesite. It can represent an immediate vent for extreme grief. Sometimes, as in the case of Sean's tampering with his friend's shoe, the task involves an intricate physical operation that can be very soothing to the performer. Grief therapists recognize an excessive restless energy that is difficult to channel as a common symptom of acute grief in its early stages. The beau geste provides the mourner with an action or a task with personal symbolic significance to perform, although the actual performance itself may appear trivial to an observer or confidante.

Later ritual actions tend to become detached from the burial site, taking place rather in locations allowing the mourner to relinquish an item of symbolic significance to the elements: the item is burned, left behind, set out to sea, or dropped into a body of water. These late-occurring actions seem to consign the items to the cosmos, signaling a reconciliation to the loss and readiness to resume normal life. In one instance recounted to me, the sister of a man who had died kept his tobacco pipes long after she had disposed of his other belongings. She finally made a little boat for them out of cardboard covered with aluminum foil and put them out to sea on his birthday. The burning of love letters, that sturdy cliché of country music, represents a similar statement of renunciation not only embodied in song but, not infrequently, acted out in life.

These ad hoc tie-breaking actions are particularly common among, though not exclusive to, those who have lost a spouse. One widow told me of tearfully dropping her first wedding ring into the ocean after she had agreed to marry again. Likewise, author Sheldon Vanauken dropped the wedding and keepsake rings he had given his wife into the Atlantic two years after her death, while making a pilgrimage to their one-time home in England.[6] These gestures of relinquishment may do more than simply mark a stage in the grieving process—they may facilitate the process itself. Anthropologists Paul C. Rosenblatt, R. Patricia Walsh, and Douglas A. Jackson have examined tie-breaking customs and ceremonies for widows and widowers cross-culturally, discovering that in cultures where such customs are highly formalized and well-entrenched, remarriage of the remaining partner is far more likely.[7]

On a practical as well as psychological level, private rituals of grief can not only express a mental state but creatively resolve a number of practical and emotional dilemmas common to those who grieve. The very diversity of needs and personal ingenuity employed in devising a beau geste ensure

that the functions as well as the forms will vary greatly from one instance to the next.

For some mourners the problem resolved is practical as well as emotional—how to dispose of items that belonged to the dead. In mainstream American culture, where no specific disposition of belongings is prescribed before or after death, the informal solution is often the Salvation Army or its equivalent for all but a few intimately personal items. These few items can represent a difficult dilemma for survivors, especially because the items themselves typically have little monetary or aesthetic value—a much-loved jacket, for example, too worn to be given to a special friend but too dense with memories to be consigned to the trashbin. Sometimes these items will be kept for several years, before they are ceremoniously "released."

The private nature of the "beau geste" can provide a mourner respite from demands that he or she return prematurely to a "normal" state of mind. There is a popular tendency in this country to underestimate the length of the grieving process, which may take several years before the mourner is prepared to resume full activities.[8] Private rituals of grief allow an individual to prolong the "griefwork" in secret beyond the unrealistically short period often expected by family and friends. Ann Landers, adviser to the lovelorn, received a letter from a fan who read the column aloud nightly to her husband, who had died the year before.[9] Likewise, a Missouri widow explained to me that for five years following her husband's death she continued to set a place for him at dinner—at first every night, later on special occasions such as his birthday or their anniversary. At these meals she would chat with her husband, bringing him up to date on family events and other happenings. She kept this a secret from family and friends at the time, only admitting it to them after some years had passed and she had remarried.

The beau geste can represent an implicit attempt to continue a relationship after death, sometimes symbolically compensating for some perceived failure or shortcoming in the performer's past treatment of the dead person. Rossetti suffered deeply from guilt over his wife's death from an overdose of laudanum. According to Oscar Wilde, Rossetti had become increasingly exasperated with Elizabeth's moodiness. One evening when they returned from dinner, Rossetti thrust a bottle of laudanum into her hands, telling her to "Take the lot!"[10] The dramatic sacrifice of the unique copies of his poems buried with her represented, in part, an attempt to atone for the misery of their marriage.

In the case of Corinne D., because her lover had been legally married to his estranged wife at the time of his death, Corinne had no part in the funeral arrangements. She had no official role as mourner and, in addition, felt partially responsible for the success of his suicide. The placement of the ring with his body represented an expression of her love for him; the secrecy of the request and the state of the shattered ring symbolized their unsanctioned and troubled love affair. "It felt right," she told me, "that it should be buried with him—some part of us."

There are instances where a beau geste represents not only an act of love and relationship but also an expression of anger or exclusion directed at other survivors, who are perceived as outsiders, ignorant of aspects of the dead person's real personality. Corinne D.'s burial of the ring with her lover was an expression of tenderness and atonement toward him, but it can also be interpreted as a discreet challenge to those whose official relationship with him allowed them special rights over his body in death but excluded her. In a similar instance of symbolic subversion, a man who had lived a creative and unconventional life was given so rigidly conventional a funeral that his brother plotted a harmless rebellion, conspiring to have him buried in a respectable suit but in his tattered and beloved sneakers—invisible, of course, beneath the hood of the casket but a source of comfort, even glee, to those few who were in on the secret.

The patterns of meaning and action apparent in the beau geste conform to those "laws of traditional behavior" identified by anthropologists and folklorists from Sir James George Frazer's time until the present.[11] The personally composed ritual of grief is often consciously modeled on an action that the subject has heard, read about, or participated in—examples abound in films, television shows, and books as well as in traditional narrative. There is, however, a real reluctance to acknowledge any specific source for the action. This desire for secrecy seems to derive from the fear of being misunderstood, combined with the sense that the inclusion is an intimate act between the dead and the living person, not to be shared indiscriminately with others. This is particularly true in episodes such as those of Corinne and Sean, in which their relationships with the deceased had been vulnerable to negative judgment before their lovers' deaths.

Participants prefer to say that the idea "just came to them." They may allude to having read or heard of similar actions by others, but they still regard their own private ritual as special, unique, and even strange to the point of being potentially misunderstood as bizarre or pathological. In cases recounted to me in Washington, D.C., and Missouri, the individuals almost invariably indicate that they consider their action to be their own in a special way, not typical of their community's expectations regarding behavior of the bereaved.

Because of the secrecy which often surrounds the performance of these actions, I might never have heard of many of them were it not for another striking aspect of the beau geste. Although it is almost always enacted privately, within it there is an additional performance component that can be realized when the individual eventually decides to recount the action. This narrative component conforms in many respects to the definition folklorist Carl von Sydow offered for the genre of folk narrative he called the *memorate:* a personal experience story that may be retold and reshaped by future narrators in traditionally determined contours, perhaps eventually evolving into a community's legend.[12] I maintain, however, that these accounts represent a singular variety of memorate. They do not recount an episode passively experienced but rather recount a conscious and purposeful enactment: an event shaped by the imagination of the narrator before its performance and then reshaped by memory and the requirements of good storytelling when it is finally shared with a listener. The narrator of an account of this kind plays multiple roles—he writes and produces the play, so to speak, then synopsizes it for a select audience.

When someone decides to tell about a beau geste of his or her own, the story is usually reserved for a carefully chosen listener who is made to feel as though party to a secret. The listener is frequently asked not to tell members of the narrator's family or community "because they'll think I'm crazy." Often this uncertainty concerning the appropriateness of the retelling is signaled by such statements as "you'll probably think I'm nuts" or "this will sound sort of weird." Sometimes qualifiers will be employed defining the narrator's self-perception: "I'm a very emotional person," "I was crazy with grief," or simply "That's just the sort of person I am." Yet while qualifying the action and performance as unusual, the narrator is seldom entirely self-deprecatory: there is a sense of pride and completion in the telling, conveying the narrator's conviction that the action was beautiful and appropriate, although liable to be misconstrued.

The narratives are often elaborately framed and carefully crafted, representing as much creative effort as did the act itself. Elements of surprise and drama are controlled to create the strongest possible effect. There is usually an effort to explain to the listener why the action chosen was an appropriate one in light of the character of the dead person, his or her special relationship with the narrator, and the significance of the role played by any symbolic items in the beau geste. There may as well be a conscious or unconscious polemical intention, as in the case of following the narrative, emerging as it did in the course of an interview on furtrapping in the Ozarks.

The speaker, Billy W., is a devoted and

conscientious trapper, head of the local organization that promotes legal and ethical trapping practices among its members. He is concerned about the misperceptions of his pastime, which he feels are at work in the legal efforts to eliminate trapping in this country. In his region, trapping has a long history, and participants almost invariably learn the skill from an older man who serves as mentor. Billy W., whose father died when he was quite young, learned from an older trapper who himself died a few years ago.

At that time, we had become such good friends that when I saw him dying of cancer, when trapping season rolled around in 1980, I said, "Bill Don, I'm not going to trap unless you can trap," and he said, "Son, I didn't teach you everything I know to see you quit now." He said, "I'm gonna die, we all have to die sometime, and you continue the tradition, like we've done for hundreds of years." And after I got to thinking about it—it took me a while, Erika, because every time I'd go down there to set a trap in the places that he'd set, I felt a . . . well, I'm a very sentimental person. So when I went I always set a trap for him, and I'd use his nametag on the trap . . .[*laughs*]

and seemed like all the places I set that trap, I always caught something the first night.

In recounting Bill Don's final insistence that he continue trapping, and the symbolic gesture that affirmed the younger man's obedience and his sense of carrying on in the tradition taught him by the older, Billy W. conveyed much in little space concerning the importance that this activity has for him personally, and for the other men of his region who engage in it.

In some instances, the eventual recounting of the action may represent a secondary symbolic tie-breaking for the narrator, in a sense reliving as well as retelling the initial beau geste, but in an emotional context beyond the primary stages of grieving. It has been suggested to me that in mainstream American cultures, beau geste narrations used as indications of a tie now effectively broken may serve as a means of establishing intimacy in the early stages of courtship among widows and widowers—a way of expressing both appropriate acknowledgment of feeling for the spouse lost and a readiness to move on in another relationship.

The recounting of a beau geste often occurs at later periods of transition in an individual's life—sometimes at the end of that life. The memory of personal rituals of bereavement can become a resource for those who, like the Anglo-Saxon councillor, are unsure what lies in the future. Because most of my work in the hospice and hospital has been with cancer patients, I have heard a number of beau geste accounts from patients who themselves were dying: cancer often allows a patient considerable time to reflect on his or her life story, and to consider the deaths of family and friends in the new light of an enforced consciousness of mortality.

Remembering the rituals that made their losses bearable, patients can find ways to think about their own impending deaths that make the prospect a less severe banishment to the unknown cold outside—the rituals are symbolic reassurance that love can defy if not conquer death. More practically, patients can use beau geste accounts to control the emotional climate surrounding them.

Annie B.'s Pentecostal family believed passionately that their prayers could bring about a miracle that would heal her medically incurable lung cancer. They would gather around her bed and conduct fervent prayer sessions, laying hands on her and speaking in tongues, alternately shouting praise and pleading for her restored health. She recounted the following story to me in the course of a conversation alone; later, I heard her tell it again and allude to it twice more in the presence of her family.

[Interviewer had just asked if the patient has ever tended a member of her family through a long illness.]

Looord yes! My mama was sick for the longest time. Months and months. And I looked after her at home, and then in the hospital. She was sick in her blood, you know, and her kidneys wouldn't work right they said.

[Was the patient's mother afraid at all while she was sick?]

Honey, she was never afraid of nothing that I ever knew. She just hated to burden us. But I'll tell you something—and it's something I never will forget, and I think of it a lot now—she got into a coma in the hospital, and the doctor said she was like' to die most any time. And we were all gathered, all her children, and her grandchildren, and praying for a healing on her. And she's been in this coma for a little less than a week, and they said she wouldn't be coming out outside of a miracle from God.

So I was with her—the rest were gone somewheres—and just holding of her hands a little and kind of talking to her. And suddenly! she gives my hand a squeeze! and opens her eyes and looks up at me! And I was never so surprised, all I could say, I just said, kinda mad, "Mama! Where've you been?" (I knew it was silly, but I was so surprised.) And she just looked up at me (her eyes were real bright) and she said: "Girl—I been looking at the heavenly paradise. I seen it. And you know—the streets *are* paved all with gold. And there's the prettiest roses just everywhere you look."

Well, I ran and got the others, and she was weak but awake for a bit, and then she settled on down to sleep and then she died later on that night. And in the morning my brother and me went on to home—this was in late March, you understand, not even Easter yet—and as we drove up the way we saw Mama's rosebush, and it had bloomed—there was three or four of the prettiest roses you ever saw on it.

Well, we kinda took that as a sign. And we picked those flowers and made a little bouquet and had them put it in Mama's hands when they buried her. And we planted a little rosebush on her grave, and it's there yet. Some folks might think it was strange, but it just seemed like the right thing to do.

[Does it bloom in March?]

[Laughs] Naw, honey. But I'll tell you this, I always do look!

Annie B. believed that prayer had the power to heal, but she was also deeply reconciled to the prospect of her own death. Her greatest concern in her last weeks was that her family recognize that her death would not be due to shortfalls of love for them on her part, invocation of grace on their part, or power on the part of the Lord. She was tired and ready for peace and quiet but reluctant to ask directly for an end to her family's prayerful intervention on her behalf. Her retelling of the story of the blooming rosebush told her family that she no longer sought a cure and did not fear death. The strenuous spiritual efforts of her family and medical efforts of the hospital staff subsided into the loving support she preferred. In telling of her mother's death and her beau geste, she taught her family how to help her die.

Every society offers its members certain rituals and patterns of behavior that are accepted as appropriate and healing. But the healing offered by such communal rites often more effectively reconciles the breach in the fabric of the community than it ministers to the private and personal needs of those whom the grief touches most nearly. Once having fulfilled the expectations of friends, family, and society with the customary funeral or memorial service, many mourners are left with a feeling that there is more to say and do. This is perhaps all the more true in the United States today, as by custom and law the tasks pertaining to care of the dying and preparation of the dead are increasingly relegated to specialists with no previous personal relationship to the individual or family.

In a sense, the beau geste derives its power from its resemblance to recognized communal rituals—and its difference from them. Its symbolism is often drawn from the language and actions of wakes, funerals, and other religious and secular cultural expressions, but it also derives its power from its contrast to such shared, communally sanctioned rites. Community rituals gain resonance from invariant repetition. The liturgy for a funeral within a given denomination does not vary much from instance to instance, except in carefully controlled portions of the service. Even funeral sermons and speeches have a formulaic sameness about them. From these consistencies the community draws a necessary comfort, in the face of the confusion compared by the Anglo-Saxon councillor to the windy cold outside the hall.

But the individuals whom loss touches most deeply often seek a separate comfort in the self-composed beau geste. Expressing the importance of one person, one relationship, one life, each beau geste is a little essay on a particular loss, quietly defying the powers in life and death that level distinction.

**NOTES**

An early version of this paper was presented at the annual meeting of the American Folklore Society, 1985, in Cincinnati, Ohio. I owe thanks to Steven Zeitlin, Jo Radnor, Ilana Abramovitch, Joseph Goodwin, and Raymond Otto for advice and encouragement.

1. J. A. Giles, ed., *The Venerable Bede's Ecclesiastical History of England* (London: Henry G. Bohn, 1849), 95.
2. Percival Christopher Wren, *Beau Geste* (New York: Grosset and Dunlap, 1924), 85.
3. Mike Royko, "A Loyal Cub Fan to the Very End," *St. Louis Post-Dispatch,* May 21, 1987, p. 4F.
4. Elisabeth Kübler-Ross, *On Children and Death* (New York: Macmillan, 1983), 7, 21.
5. Joseph Knight, *The Life of Dante Gabriel Rossetti* (Folcroft, Pennsylvania: Folcroft Library Edition, 1973), repr. 1887 ed., 76.
6. Sheldon Vanauken, *A Severe Mercy* (San Francisco: Harper and Row, 1977), 223–24.
7. Paul C. Rosenblatt, R. Patricia Walsh, and Douglas A. Jackson, *Grief and Mourning in Cross-Cultural Perspective* (Human Relations Area Files, 1976), 67–85.
8. The classic work outlining the grieving process remains Erich Lindemann, "Symptomatology and Management of Acute Grief," *American Journal of Psychiatry* 101 (1944): 141–48.
9. *St. Louis Post-Dispatch,* January 30, 1986; October 13, 1986, p. 2F.
10. Brian and Judy Dobbs, *Dante Gabriel Rossetti: An Alien Victorian* (London: Macdonald and Janes, 1977), 143.
11. For example, the use of items associated with the dead in memorializing them recalls Frazer's principle of "contagious magic." *See* Sir James George Frazer, *The Golden Bough: A Study in Magic and Religion,* abridged edition (New York: Macmillan, 1922), 43–52.
12. Carl W. von Sydow, *Selected Papers on Folklore: Published on the Occasion of his 70th Birthday,* ed. Laurits Bodker (Copenhagen: Rosenkilde and Bagger, 1948), 127–45.

# George Catlin and Karl Bodmer

## Artists among the American Indians

BY JAMES GILREATH

Map of the Western & Middle Portions of North America, To Illustrate the History of California, Oregon, and the Other Countries on the North-West Coast of America. (Detail) Drawn by George H. Ringgold, Engraved by E. F. Woodward, Philadelphia. Published in Robert Greenhow's History of Oregon and California, 1844. Geography and Map Division

In the early spring of 1832, George Catlin, a self-taught American portrait painter with a modest reputation, packed his art supplies and headed up the Missouri River from St. Louis on the American Fur Company's steamboat, the *Yellowstone*. A little more than a year later, Prince Maximilian, owner of an estate on the Rhone River near the town of Coblenz, in what is now West Germany, departed St. Louis on the same steamer. To document his journey, Maximilian hired Karl Bodmer, a trained Swiss artist whose specialty was landscape painting. The wilderness along the Missouri River in North and South Dakota was familiar only to native Indians and fur trappers in the early 1830s. The American Fur Company had established forts along the river to facilitate trading. However, the company's business was acquiring pelts, not sharing knowledge.

Catlin and the Maximilian-Bodmer party charted almost identical paths into the American West. Catlin followed the Missouri for almost two thousand miles from St. Louis to Fort Union at the confluence of the Yellowstone and Missouri Rivers, near the present Montana and North Dakota border. He reached the fort during the summer of 1832 and remained for about two months to paint in oils the Blackfeet and Crow Indians who camped nearby. Before returning to St. Louis by canoe, he stopped for a month at Fort Clark to visit the Mandans. Some of Catlin's most remarkable paintings were produced during this time. His resolute persistence in the face of hazards and uncertain conditions was remarkable.

Maximilian and Bodmer reached New Harmony in Indiana during the autumn of 1832. The New Harmony community was founded seven years earlier by British philanthropist Robert Owen to promote two socialist objectives—the equal division of labor and the common ownership of property. After spending the winter with the Owenites, they resumed their journey in April 1833. The group traveled by steamer to Fort Union, where the year before, after spending the summer, Catlin had turned back. But Maximilian and Bodmer pushed further west and covered the next five hundred miles by keelboat. As the expedition moved along the river, it frequently stopped to dispatch hunting parties, at times becoming a combination of scientific exploration and gentleman's adventure. Bodmer was assigned to paint likenesses of the surrounding landscape and of the animals the hunters brought back to camp. At the forts, his attention switched to making portraits of visiting Indians. They endured a brutal winter at the desolate outpost of Fort Mackenzie. During the spring of 1834, with Maximilian very sick, the group backtracked to St. Louis and by the summer had left New York, never to return to America.

Despite the similarity of Catlin's and Bodmer's routes, their attitudes about their work markedly differed. Catlin set out to preserve a record of what he considered a superior but vanishing race. He admiringly

wrote that among the frontier Indians he found "the proud and chivalrous pale of savage society, in the state of original nature, beyond the reach of civilized contamination." He set as his mission to become the historian of the tribes and several times abandoned his family for long periods. He immersed himself in Indian culture and once commented that he had "become so much an Indian of late that my pencil has lost all appetite for subjects that savor of tameness." For Catlin, the Indians were a foil to the rapidly accelerating complexities of the nineteenth century. One also suspects that his devotion to a great historic quest was at least in part an attempt to palliate the disappointments in his earlier professional career. The intensity of his ideological enthusiasm spills over into Catlin's writing. He claimed to have composed one of his books at the "urgent request of a number of my friends." Catlin worked quickly on the canvases, sometimes leaving details to be filled in at a later date. This method caused some inaccuracies. He is at his best in catching groups of Indians in motion in ritual dance ceremonies. His work shows the Missouri River Indians to be part of a lively and complex culture. This was an important point to make at a time when European philosophical writers such as Cornelius de Pauw and Comte Georges Louis Leclerc de Buffon were saying that all species of life in America were weak and inferior because of the hostile environment.

In contrast, Bodmer's paintings were not an attempt to convey an ideological position. He was a paid scientific illustrator, not a social commentator. Documenting the expedition's progress was his job. When he hired Bodmer, Prince Maximilian commented favorably that the Swiss painter could "draw what was put in front of him." The prince wanted to record information that might help those who were trying to understand the origins and histories of the world's races. Consequently, Bodmer spent less time on the dramatic aspects of the tribes he encountered. Even his landscapes are quieter and more reflective than Catlin's. With only a few exceptions, the Swiss artist's work is dispassionate, even at its most beautiful and ethnologically exact.

The dispositions of Catlin's and Maximilian's collections of paintings, Indian artifacts, and animal specimens gathered during their trips proved to be as different as the two men's backgrounds. Catlin exhibited his collection in several American cities and tried to interest Congress in purchasing it. Failing in this, he shipped everything to England, rented Egyptian Hall in London, and charged visitors an entrance fee. Later, he took the material on a European tour. Commissions for paintings, profits from books, and admission to his exhibit were his only means of support. His championing of the Indian as representative natural man was inextricably bound with his need to make a living. For Maximilian, profit was not a motive. Except for a few paintings he allowed Bodmer to keep, Maximilian retained control of the material, and it remained in his family's castle until it was purchased in the early 1960s by InterNorth, Inc., of Omaha, Nebraska.

Both Catlin and Maximilian decided to publicize their travels by publishing color-plate books based on paintings done in the field. In the eighteenth and nineteenth centuries, before the age of photography, color-plate books were the most realistic way to document discoveries and to record natural history observations in book form. Such works consisted of groups of engravings, etchings, aquatints, woodcuts, or lithographs that were meant to be bound together and hand-colored. Usually, the colorists followed a model so that there was a general consistency between the same print as found in different copies of the same edition. Of course, there were many individual variations due to such factors as differing degrees of talent among those doing the coloring. The atlas of illustrations based on Bodmer's paintings was sold in Germany with *Reise in das innere Nord-America,* a report of the trip published between 1839 and 1841; with a French edition of the text in 1840–43; and with an English translation in 1843. Purchasers could acquire the prints colored, uncolored, or in a mixture of both. Catlin's *North American Indian Portfolio* was issued in London in 1844 and in New York the following year. Both books were financed by their authors, but the fact that Catlin did not have Maximilian's wealth meant that the American's job was much more difficult.

It is fortunate for our understanding of Indian folkways that Catlin and Maximilian began their work when they did. Though the tribes of the Missouri River region were remote, they were not isolated. Nor were their cultures static. Indian parties journeyed to St. Louis, Philadelphia, and Washington, inevitably changing the travelers' outlooks. One Indian sojourner who returned to his village after a trip to Washington was shunned as a liar by the rest of his tribe for reporting about such things as ships and balloons that they thought too incredible to be believed. Traders were also powerful forces in altering Indian cultural patterns. These early changes were modest compared to the revolutionary restructuring of Indian society caused by later American emigration. The Mandans were almost totally obliterated by a small-pox epidemic not long after Catlin and Maximilian left their village. Popular books such as the *Leatherstocking Tales* and imaginary Indian captivity narratives had created false images of the Indian as either a noble savage or satanic devil that were rooted in sales figures, not in accurate visual representation. The magnificent, hand-colored illustrations of Maximilian's *Reise in das innere Nord-America* and George Catlin's *North American Indian Portfolio*, a few of which are reproduced to accompany this essay, were instrumental in changing this situation. These picture books, based on personal experience and produced in a very limited number of copies, were meant for an elite audience and were not guided by popular prejudice in the United States.

Bodmer's pictures in *Reise in das innere Nord-America* are esthetically more satisfying than Catlin's illustrations. However, the fierce independence and driving individuality that earmarked all of Catlin's efforts

and were necessary to bring the volume to completion are apparent in *North American Indian Portfolio*. These qualities give character and vigor to the book at its best moments. That sense of personality is not found in Bodmer's work as realized in Maximilian's book. Bodmer did not even have the opportunity to choose which of his pictures were to be represented. Bodmer's work is more beautiful and technically proficient, but Catlin's is more expressive. Though the emotive dimension of *North American Indian Portfolio* is sometimes idiosyncratic, it is the underlying reason the book is an interpretative triumph.

SUGGESTED READING

An early account of Catlin's life that is readable but outdated on some points is George McCracken's *George Catlin and the Old Frontier* (New York: Dial Press, 1959), which has recently been republished by Bonanza Books. Catlin's account of his trip, *Letters and Notes on the Manners, Customs, and Condition of the North American Indians,* has been reprinted in paperback (New York: Dover, 1973). His narrative of the European tour of his exhibition, *Catlin's Notes of Eight Years' Travels and Residence in Europe, With His North American Indian Collection,* has not been in print since the nineteenth century but is widely available at research libraries. The most comprehensive and best look at Catlin and his works is William Truettner's *The Natural Man Observed* (Washington: Smithsonian Institution Press, 1979). Truettner also takes a critical look at the selection of images in Catlin's colorplate book in an article "For European Audiences: Catlin's *North American Indian Portfolio*" in Ron Tyler's *Prints of the American West* (Fort Worth: Amon Carter Museum, 1983).

The original English-language translation of Prince Maximilian's report was reprinted as *Maximilian's, Prince of Wied's, Travels in the Interior of North America, 1832–1834* in 1906 as volumes 22 through 25 of Reuben Gold Thwaites's *Early Western Travels* series. The translation is incomplete and the University of Oklahoma Press is sponsoring a new one. The best book on the expedition is *Karl Bodmer's America* (Lincoln: Joslyn Art Museum and University of Nebraska Press, 1984). It has an introductory essay by William H. Goetzmann and annotations for the numerous illustrations by David C. Hunt and Marsha V. Gallagher. There is a biography of Bodmer by William J. Orr included in the volume. George P. Tomko's "The Western Prints of Karl Bodmer" in Ron Tyler's *Prints of the American West* discusses the classical allusions in Bodmer's work.

*The Snow-Shoe Dance. Plate 14 in George Catlin's* North American Indian Portfolio.
*Rare Book and Special Collections Division*

*Catlin witnessed the Snow-Shoe Dance of the Chippeway or Ojibway Indians who had gathered near Fort Snelling, Minnesota. The dancers sang thanks for the first snowfall. Snowshoes, which the performers wore during the entire ceremony, enabled the Indians to track and pursue game easily when the ground was covered with deep snow.*

*Buffalo Dance. Plate 8 in George Catlin's* North American Indian Portfolio. *Rare Book and Special Collections Division*

*The Mandan Indians performed the Buffalo Dance every spring to lure bison to their villages. Unlike larger and more powerful tribes, the Mandans did not roam extensively to hunt. Wearing buffalo heads and hides, participants in the dance chanted and continuously circled until they were exhausted. When a dancer leaned forward to signal his weariness, he was shot with a blunt arrow. Spectators dragged him by his heels away from the other dancers and pretended to skin him with knives. The ceremony did not stop until a herd wandered into the vicinity. The buffalo was a crucial source of food, clothing, and shelter for the Mandans and other Plains Indians.*

*Ball-Play Dance. Plate 22 in George Catlin's* North American Indian Portfolio. *Rare Book and Special Collections Division*

*Catlin encountered the Choctaws near Fort Gibson, to which they had been forced to move from their native lands in northern Alabama and Mississippi. He was impressed by their ability to preserve in their new home such traditional customs as the Ball-Play Dance. As many as a thousand Indians gathered as contestants, and many more massed nearby to watch. Before the ball was tossed into play, the opposing teams huddled near their goals to dance, shout, and knock their sticks together. Women, who had wagered household goods on the outcome, formed parallel lines between the groups to cheer on the players.*

*Ball Play. Plate 23 in George Catlin's* North American Indian Portfolio. *Rare Book and Special Collections Division*

In this game players cradled the ball in the webbing of their rackets while running or passed it to a teammate. A ball thrown or carried between the stakes of the goal counted as a score. Anything that prevented the ball carrier from moving toward the goal was allowed. Fights broke out away from the center of action, making the entire field a melee. One hundred points were needed to win.

*Bison-Dance of the Mandans. Tableau 18 in Prince Maximilian Alexander Philipp von Wied-Neuwied's* Reise in das innere Nord-America in den Jahren 1832 bis 1834. *Rare Book and Special Collections Division*

*Karl Bodmer, the artist who accompanied Maximilian, made the Buffalo Dance the subject of one of his liveliest paintings. His depiction is more detailed than Catlin's. Bodmer observed that only the two bravest hunters of the Buffalo Clan were permitted to wear the entire head during the dance. The rest wore only the horns and part of the mane.*

*Scalp Dance of the Minatarres. Tableau 27 in Prince Maximilian Alexander Philipp von Wied-Neuwied's* Reise in das innere Nord-America in den Jahren 1832 bis 1834. *Rare Book and Special Collections Division*

*The Hidatsa tribe—or Minatarres as Maximilian called them—celebrated a war victory with the Scalp Dance. Warriors who took a scalp in battle presented it to a woman as a sign of respect. The honored women then performed this dance, holding the scalps at the end of long poles.*

*Pehriska-Ruhpa. Tableau 28 in Prince Maximilian Alexander Philipp von Wied-Neuwied's*
Reise in das innere Nord-America in den Jahren 1832 bis 1834. *Rare Book and Special*
*Collections Division*

---

*This plate shows a leader of one of the Hidatsa Dog Societies in a magnificent ceremonial*
*costume. Members of the Real Dog Society were expected to be daring and brave in battle.*
*Other Hidatsa Dog Clans were the Crazy Dogs, the Little Dogs, the Dogs-Whose-Names-*
*Are-Unknown, and the Old Dogs.*

*Dance of the Mandan Women. Vignette 28 in Prince Maximilian Alexander Philipp von Wied-Neuwied's* Reise in das innere Nord-America in den Jahren 1832 bis 1834. *Rare Book and Special Collections Division*

---

*The White Buffalo Society was the most important Mandan women's religious group. One of its principal functions was the presentation of a dance to attract buffaloes to the village. All the dancers wore turbans made from buffalo hides, and the leader of the society dressed in a white buffalo robe, which was thought to convey great power. The women dancers moved in a circle with a duck-like walk to the accompaniment of male singers.*

# American Indian Powwow

BY VANESSA BROWN
and BARRE TOELKEN

*The Crow Fair campgrounds, August 1979. The circle is an important symbol of unity at the powwow and manifests itself in the shape of the arena and in the dances that take place there. (MT9-MC20-8) Photograph by Michael S. Crummett*

A lthough the intertribal powwow has developed rapidly since the turn of the century as a common form of Native American social expression and is now to be found in every state of the union, surprisingly little has been written about it. Anthropologists and folklorists seem to have avoided the subject as a newer form of expression that does not represent a pure tribal strain of folk or ethnic tradition (an ironic opinion, if it indeed persists, for the subject of "purity" in tradition has not occupied the theoretical musings of folklorists for some years now). Perhaps because cash prizes are involved and non-Indians are encouraged to attend, some may consider the phenomenon to be more a part of popular culture than of folk tradition. Whatever the reason, the powwow has not produced a rich scholarship.

This essay draws upon our own experiences with the powwow as it exists in the West and the northern Plains and is written from the dual perspectives of a Native

American who dances in powwows and helps organize them and a folklorist who studies traditional performance events. We will not pretend to give a comprehensive account of the genre, however, for even in the West there are large regional differences in the singing and the dancing protocol.

The term *powwow* seems to come from one of the Algonquin languages (Northeastern America), where it originally meant a medicine man or conjurer. The term was borrowed by the white Europeans to refer not only to a medicine man but to a meeting at which curing took place. Eventually it was used by the whites to denote virtually any gathering of Indians, especially where singing might take place. Indians have borrowed back this term (and several others used in the powwow—like *war dance*) from English usage.

Today a powwow is essentially a social dance where Indian people from several tribes dance together, using a few basic pat-terns that all the tribes recognize. The music is highly stylized, and the dancing goes on most of the afternoon and evening, with the dancers resting occasionally while particular groups (young men or older women, for example) compete for prize money. From time to time, the hosts or a visiting group will demonstrate a particular dance from their own tribe while other participants watch. Visitors are welcome, but non-Indians are sometimes asked to pay an entrance fee, which helps to support the cost of the event and to pay for the prizes awarded for dancing. The powwow is a social event stressing intertribal affiliations more than tribal differences and displaying traditional Indian characteristics as well as innovations.

There are two major settings for the powwow: one is the outdoor encampment, sometimes called a fair, which lasts from three days to a week, and at which people live in a traditional Indian-style tent village. These

outdoor encampments are so large that they require a camp crier or caller, a man mounted on horseback (sometimes today riding in a small truck with a loudspeaker system), who circulates through the camp to announce camp regulations and the times the dances will take place. Smaller powwows last only one or two days and are often held indoors. The outdoor powwow is usually held on or near an Indian reservation, while the smaller powwows are also held in the cities where urban Indians or students far from home organize them in order to invite their reservation friends and families to dance.

Although the dancing arena in both cases is circular, the large outdoor encampment has tents around the outside perimeter of the area and a brush arbor or pavilion in the very center in which the dancing takes place. A number of large drums, around which five to ten singers and drummers may be seated, are placed in the center, and the dancing takes place around them. Some-

times they are arranged around the perimeter of this pavilion, and the dancing takes place in the middle. In the urban powwows, which are often held in a basketball court or some similarly large indoor area, the drums are usually arranged down the center of the room, and the dancers move around them in an elongated oval.

The closing of a powwow will vary somewhat depending on whether it is indoors or outdoors, and whether it is the last night or not. When urban Indians rent a hall or a basketball court for their powwow, they must obey regulations about the closing of the building. When it is clear that only fifteen or twenty minutes remain, the master of ceremonies usually announces a round dance, followed by an intertribal war dance, and then everyone leaves. At an outdoor powwow, the ending may come when the weather becomes too cold, when too few people are left, or when too few drums are available for the dancing to go on. On the last night of a powwow, there are usually several honoring dances, and these are arranged so that there is a more ritualistic sense of closure for the entire powwow. None of this is controlled by formal time schedules, except insofar as the group must adhere to regulations for vacating a hall. Otherwise, the powwow dynamic is one in which the numerical build-up of people eventually brings about the activity, and then their disappearance at the end signals that a particular dance is the last one.

Planning for either kind of powwow may begin several months or even a year ahead of time. Committees organized by tribal governments, by smaller clubs and associations within a tribe, or by a group of Indian students at a university will start making plans and sending invitations to other Indian groups on and off reservations. A good many Indian groups present powwows annually, and the planning group need only determine the date, which is almost always arrived at in consultation with other Native American groups who may also be giving powwows. At an outdoor powwow,

the plans include the layout of the encampment, arrangements for water and food, disposal of garbage, and the order of events. Since people bring their own food and tents with them, there is no need to plan for these. For the indoor urban powwow, both food and lodging are donated by other Indian people or by friends of Indian people who live in the nearby area. One function of the planning, then, is for a local Indian community in an urban area to reestablish and reaffirm its ties among its own members (who may be members of a variety of tribes) and to encourage friendships with other Indian communities, as well as with non-Indians who have been active in helping to encourage and support Indian observances. This is also a time for discussing older and newer ideas on style of dress, dance, and song.

In spite of the careful planning, however, the powwow unfolds more according to ancient Native American attitudes toward time and ritual than with regard to modern calendars and clocks. The powwow seems to flower of its own accord, and the dynamics are internal to the events. Of course, because most Indian people today have jobs and other obligations, the powwow indeed takes place during the week or weekend in which it is scheduled. Very often one will see an advertisement that the afternoon's dancing will start at 2:30, and that the evening events will begin at 7:30. If the observer arrives somewhat before these times in order to watch the entire sequence, he will often wait an hour or two before anything discernible happens. People begin to gather, often having come from great distances. They talk to friends and relations, renew old acquaintances, appear and disappear, change from their everyday clothing to dancing regalia, and it may be 9 or 9:30 P.M. before the evening's dances actually begin in the powwow arena. Other than dancing, the most important part of the powwow to Indian people is the social aspect of gathering together, and this is what receives most of the attention.

The men's outfits at a powwow are usually quite different from what they would wear at one of the sacred dances at home. First of all, a good many of the men will be wearing the fancy dance outfit which features colors, bird feathers, and bells. Those who are dancing in the traditional style will be clothed in deerhide or in simple trousers made from early Hudson Bay Company blankets. On the other hand, the women's clothing at a powwow is often the same that they would wear at home on any ritual occasion. Many Indian people feel that this consistency is further indication of the extent to which the dignity, grace, and power of women are demonstrated. That is to say, women do not have to wear special clothing for a powwow because they take their own tribal dignity with them wherever they go. Indeed, in many tribes it remains the women who continue to pass on language, religious belief, and other cultural instruction to the younger generation, especially since it is the custom among many tribes for the grandmother to raise the children.

Whatever the style of the outfit, straight or fancy, the production of the clothing (often as gifts from friends, relatives, or lovers) is based on beliefs and assumptions about the symbolic function of the clothing.

Outfits should include something from the Wingeds (birds, who, being two-legged like humans, are considered as close relatives), especially the feathers of an eagle. This is the bird that gets closest to the sun, the only bird who has one mate for life, the bird who takes prayers and messages to Wakan Tanka. The Four-leggeds, who also supply us with food and other necessities and provide hides for moccasins and dresses and fur for decoration, are also represented in the outfit, along with decorations placed by human hands and supplied by creatures from the waters in the form of shells. This is said to honor all that gives life on earth, all that provides humans with food, warmth, and sacred power. Wearing symbolic clothes, the dancers are one with all the living beings who share the world with them as their relatives. As people prepare or create their outfits for the powwow, stories are told and attitudes are mentioned that strengthen these symbolic recollections and pass them on to younger people, who are very much incorporated into the creative process. Thus, the outfits worn at the powwow provide an

*Contestants register for the dance competition at the 1983 Omaha powwow in Macy, Nebraska. (FCP/0-CF3-5) Photograph by Carl Fleischhauer*

occasion for the material and oral articulation and transmission of traditional values.

The most important development as the powwow gets under way is the gathering of people around the drums. Among the groups invited to a powwow there will be several groups who are expected, perhaps specifically invited, to bring a drum (the term is used both for the instrument and for the group of player-singers). A drum group from the local area may be honored by the planning committee by being asked to serve as "Host Drum." But the important thing is that people have often not decided ahead of time exactly who will drum, and a drum may not begin drumming until a proper number of drummers have decided to come forward and sit around the drum (the number varies in different tribes). When such a "critical mass" has gathered, the people around drums will then begin to sing and to practice (to "warm up"), and it is not until two or three of the drums have tested a few songs that dancers will move onto the floor and begin dancing. When it is clear that there are enough drums to allow for a sequence of dances to take place, the master of ceremonies announces the opening processional.

Each tribe has certain beliefs and customs about the use of the drum. Many tribes believe that a drum expresses the heartbeat of the people, or the heartbeat of the earth, calling everyone to listen—that it is like a living person. Drums can get sick and can be cured, and therefore they must be handled with care. In some tribes, only the males may sing while gathered directly around the drum. When women sing, it is usually by forming a small semicircle behind the men and singing in a piercing falsetto an octave above the men's voices. In some tribes, women are seated among the men at the drum, and in some tribes even

The Grand Entry begins
each dance session at the
1983 Omaha powwow, as
a dancer carrying the
American flag leads the
other participants in a
circle around the arena.
(FCP/0-CF9-6) Photograph
by Carl Fleischhauer

children are invited to join. Drummers are expected to know the songs thoroughly. Not everyone is allowed to approach the drum, and no one under the influence of drugs or alcohol is allowed anywhere close. Menstruating women are not to sing around the drum or dance, but they may attend the powwow as spectators.

Each drum (that is, each group of singers who arrange themselves around a drum) receives payment to cover the expenses of transportation. If a certain drum has been asked to sing an honoring song during the powwow, the family of the person honored will donate a gift of money to the drum. While these sums of money are usually quite modest, in the case of an honoring dance, particularly for someone recently deceased, the amount can be as much as $100. The gift is almost always announced publicly as well. Singers usually spend the entire powwow gathered at their drum, alternating with the other drums. Since in a powwow of five drums there is ample time to rest one's voice between songs, some drummers will get up and join the other dancers, especially toward the end of the evening. Whenever a round dance is called, in which all spectators and participants should take part, two or three of the drummers will be seen moving through the crowds gesturing at people with their drumsticks to come to the floor to dance.

In many Western tribes, the drum cannot begin playing until it has a certain number of people gathered around it. For example, at Warm Springs Reservation the usual number gathered around a drum is seven. The drum carrier places it on the powwow floor and then sits there with his drumsticks, talking to two or three of his friends, some of whom may also have decided to drum and sing. Slowly other people from the Warm Springs Reservation will come forward and converse briefly at the drum, and over a period of perhaps an hour or more people will sit down and pick up a drumstick, and tentatively make some light noises on the drum. When there are seven people gathered, the drum carrier, who is also the lead singer, will wait for a moment of silence from the other drums and then begin, very quietly, a warm-up song. The

other drummers at his drum will join in, and they may sing two or three songs to loosen up their vocal chords. As the evening goes on they will sing louder and louder, and there is a tremendous strain on the voice. For this reason, a number of traditional Indian medicinal plants, such as yarrow root, are used to protect the throat.

The opening ceremony includes at least a "flag dance" in which national flags of the United States and Canada are paraded around the arena, along with the Indian warriors' flag, actually a staff festooned with eagle feathers honoring Indian people who have died in warfare. Many Indian people are veterans of World Wars I and II, and many of them belong to the various official veterans' groups organized by former members of the armed services of the United States. But it is made very clear during this processional that the warriors' flag represents all warriors who have fallen in all wars, and this is a very pointed reference to the number of people who fell while fighting against European invaders. The tableau scene of the American and Canadian flags, along with the warriors' flag, in procession around the pavilion together, is somewhat ironic on the political level, but is also a reminder of the ways in which American Indians have survived culturally by amalgamating a good many of their interests with those of the countries which have surrounded them. It also stands as a symbolic cameo of the syncretic, amalgamating force of the powwow itself.

After the opening "flag song," there is often an invocation or pipe ceremony, then an "intertribal war dance," not a dance that has anything to do with war, but a dance whose steps are celebrative (which led early white observers to assume that it was a dance done only in the case of victory in war). The first half-dozen dances or so are all of the intertribal "war dance" variety and are often referred to as "warm-up dances," because of their function in getting everyone into the festivities.

Although each tribe has numerous spe-

*Crow Fair, August 1979 (MT9-MCZ6-5) Photograph by Michael Crummett*

cial dances of its own, the powwow features two kinds of dances which everyone does, plus a few others which are done by smaller numbers of participants. The two most prevalent dances are the so-called "war dance" and the "round dances." War dancing is the kind of dance in which each individual develops a particular dancing style based upon his or her regalia, some elements from his or her vision quest, or something related to family history. At the same time, however, all of these dances, no matter how individualized they may be, are done to the same beat and have essentially the same footwork. The men are expected to dance energetically, and most of them have noisemakers attached to their legs: sleighbells, various kinds of shells, and even large cowbells. The men's role in the war dance is to maintain and extend the heavy pulse of the drum, which holds all people together in dance. The women, on the other hand, dance very lightly, some of the best

seeming almost to float over the ground, for their role in these dances is to symbolize the dignity and the delicacy of the woman's position in nature. Both men and women recognize at least two kinds of war dances. For the men, there is the so-called "fancy dance" (a more contemporary style in which the dancer wears an outfit festooned with feathers and fur that provide a stunning display of color and movement as the dance proceeds) and the "straight" or traditional war dance (featuring older and simpler styles of men's clothing, reminiscent of the dress of about two hundred years ago). Fancy dancing derives mostly from the Plains Indians but is done by virtually all tribes who come to a powwow, especially for competition, because of the demanding footwork. In recent years, the straight-dance style has become popular again, and in the contests in the larger powwows today, the traditional dancers have increased to the point that they are, in some

*Parade dance at the Crow Fair, August 1979. (MT9-MC26-2) Photograph by Michael S. Crummett*

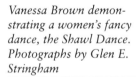

*Vanessa Brown demonstrating a women's fancy dance, the Shawl Dance. Photographs by Glen E. Stringham*

cases, more numerous than the fancy dancers.

Most of the women dance a style of war dance that would be called "traditional," both in outfit and in its dance step. Some of the younger teenage women, however, dance a fancy dance called the Shawl Dance, in which a woman wears a large shawl with long fringes that wave back and forth as she dances. The shawls of the 1800s were buffalo hides; later, woolen blankets were used, and recently fringed polyester has become popular. The footwork is spectacular and the dance is so athletic that hardly anyone over the age of twenty does it. In all of these war dances, the individual dances without a definite partner, although one often sees small groups of women (often related to each other) or groups of two or three men friends dancing together around the circle. The dancing usually moves in a clockwise or sunwise direction during a war dance, although this can vary from one powwow to another.

The other most common kind of dance is the round dance, sometimes called a friendship or unity dance, in which the dancers and the spectators arrange themselves in a huge circle side by side facing inward and

dance to a pulsating rhythm by stepping to the side and then bringing the feet together again. The circle of dancers moving round and round, often in concentric circles when the crowd is large enough, represents the bringing together of all people and is considered highly symbolic of the function of the powwow. For this reason, the round dances are not done as often as the war dances, for they are much more emotionally and culturally charged (although they are certainly not as athletic as the other dances). Round dances move in a sunwise direction, because they not only relate the participants to each other but represent the relationship of the dancers to the movements of the sun and the universe.

Other popular dances from nearby tribes may also be done. For example, at the Flathead Indian powwow at Arlee, Montana, Indian people from Oklahoma may be asked to lead a dance called the "Oklahoma Two-step." The lead couple, holding hands, run around the arena followed by other dancers, also in couples. The lead couple may stop and dance in place, may jump up and down, may run backwards, may split off with men and women going in different directions to come together at another part of the pavilion, and so on, all to the tune of a very rapid beat. All participants must follow the actions of the lead couple, and usually the dance dissolves in laughter as people begin tripping over each other and falling to the ground.

At any time an article of clothing from a dancer's regalia is lost or dropped on the floor, its return to the owner must be ritualized. Minor items such as a bell or a pair of glasses may simply be turned in or re-ported to the master of ceremonies, but something like an eagle feather calls for an ornate and serious ceremony. Naturally, there are regional and tribal variations on this ritual, but as it is typically seen in the West, the Whipman—one of the chosen officials on the dance floor—stands by the feather to make sure no one dances on it. After the conclusion of the dance in progress, the lost feather is announced, and a Lost Feather dance is quickly arranged. It usually calls for the four best male dancers to surround the feather and dance around it and up to it almost as if they were hunting an animal. Just before they reach the feather, the changing beat of the drums calls them back to the perimeters of their circle, and the hunting starts again. Finally,

*Grand Entry at the 1983 Omaha powwow. The dancing of the women is characterized by dignity and grace. (FCP/0-DSL3-13) Photograph by Dorothy Sara Lee*

after some minutes of dancing, one of the dancers (sometimes the person who actually noticed the feather first, but nearly always a war veteran in any case) dances up to the feather, picks it up and holds it over his head with a triumphant whoop, at which all dancers then circle the pavilion sunwise. The owner is asked to come forward and claim the feather, then narrate a story about how it was first obtained and what relationship it bears to the dancer's regalia or the dancer. The owner will often sing a song or play a drum to honor the person who found and recovered the precious feather. In some powwows, all lost objects are dealt with in this way, partly to show publicly that a missing item was not stolen or misused, and partly because it calls the loss to the attention of the owner who, in a large crowd, may not have noticed a part of regalia falling and might not have heard an announcement over the loudspeaker.

During any powwow, several honoring dances may be done which call attention to the survivors of calamities, to the anniversary of some well-known person's death, to the services and values of old people, or to graduates of local high schools and colleges. During an honoring dance, one drum is asked to play a slow war dance, and the person or persons being honored dance sunwise around the pavilion all alone. On the second time around, close friends and family members may join in behind, and as the dance continues all dancers fall into place until the entire pavilion has become a parade. This is another example of the still-widespread Native American idea that dancing is far more than entertaining fun; rather, when we dance with other people, we place ourselves gesturally and symbolically into patterns that relate us to all people on a deeper level.

The hosts of a powwow may begin a powwow with one of their own special dances by way of welcoming participants. Every eight or ten years, for example, at the Arlee (Montana) powwow, the Flathead people do their Snake Dance, which is a

long processional dance beginning far out
in the tipi village that surrounds the dance
area, moves single-file through the tipis,
and eventually arrives at the powwow
grounds. Only Flatheads take part in this
dance, and it is said to derive from a time in
which a Flathead who had been bitten by
a snake was cured when the whole tribe
danced the snake's dance. Occasionally this
dance is done in celebration of the relationship between Flathead Indians and the
snakes (whose appearance and disappearance during the year are also calendar signs
indicating when certain stories may be told
or not told). The Warm Springs Indians
usually offer to do a Butterfly Dance, in
which four to ten teenage girls dance in
a very limited step with their blankets
wrapped around their shoulders and heads

with their bodies bent over. In this part of
the dance, they represent the worm or the
cocoon of a butterfly, and later when the
dance's rhythm changes to something more
energetic, the girls begin doing a much
more active step. They throw their arms
and blankets back, using the blankets as if
they were wings, and whirl around in large
circles celebrating the movement of nature
from cocoon to butterfly, and also, of
course, symbolizing the movement of a
young girl to womanhood. The Hoop
Dance, once done mostly by the Southwest
Indians, has now been taken up by young
men of many tribes, and may be done as an
exhibition. In this dance some five to seven
hoops less than one meter in diameter are
placed on the ground in a row and the
dancer dances up to them, steps on their

edges, and causes them to move up his legs and around his body until finally all hoops are in use, whirling on the dancer's arms or forming patterns as he interlocks his arms with them.

The Tolowa Indians in northern California and southern Oregon do a Deer Dance, in which the dancers simply stand in a line and bend rhythmically at the knees while small deer hooves attached to their costumes click together in rhythm. The dance is done as an exhibition and only the Tolowa do it. Such exhibition dances are only those that may be done away from home ground and under more or less secular circumstances. Almost all of these tribes have other sacred dances that must only be done at home (one thinks of the Yeibichei Dance and the so-called Squaw Dance of the Navajos, the Snake and Antelope ceremony of the Hopis, or the Brush Dance and the White Deerskin Ceremony of the Hupa). These and many other tribal dances are tied deeply to certain areas of land, sacred spots, or particular villages, and they are considered very much in the nature of religious worship. For these reasons, such dances are not normally done at powwows, although sometimes at intertribal ceremo-

nials members of these tribes will show a few steps of the dance to spectators.

It is clear that the Native American powwow selects those dances that people of different tribes can watch or learn and do together without intruding on each other's religious beliefs; and the special dances from particular tribes are chosen so as to minimize the possibility of misuse. This testifies to an ongoing sensitivity about the dance and its importance in the lives of the people themselves. For fun, some powwow announcers will ask all Indians to leave the floor so the non-Indian visitors can be honored by being taught the "Wanabee Dance" (afterward explained as a dance for those who "wanabee" Indians).

At the same time the dancing occurs, other things of traditional but lesser importance are also taking place. For one thing, food is prepared and sold around the periphery of the dancing—especially the favorite Indian snack, fry-bread. This is made by flattening a piece of bread dough into a circle about the size of a small plate and

*Below left: Luanna White beading buckskin chaps at the Montana powwow, 1979, while nephews Todd Wilson and Steven White play and sleep nearby. (MT9-MC23-16) Photograph by Michael S. Crummett*

*Below right: Near the powwow arena, beads, jewelry, and Indian crafts are offered for sale. Omaha powwow, 1983. (FCP/0-CF6-14) Photograph by Carl Fleischhauer*

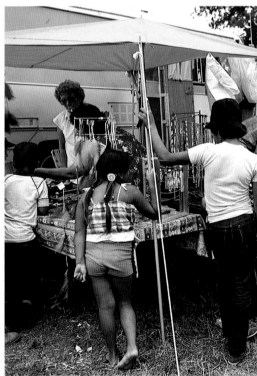

dropping it into boiling fat or grease. This bread was not an original staple of the American Indians, but it is one of the ways in which Indians learned to make food with the flour given to them by the government in payment for some of their lands. Since much of the flour was infested with worms and insects, the Indians needed to find both a way to cook it and a way to kill its various passengers. Today, of course, fry-bread is made with regular commercial flour, but it has become not only a treat but a reminiscence of the days of early subjugation to the whites. Also around the periphery of the powwow arena there will be booths displaying beads, jewelry, furs, and any number of arts and crafts which Indian people have brought with them to offer in trade or sale to other Indians (or to non-Indian spectators). Teenagers meet, talk, and flirt. Circulating on the periphery of the dancing area in order to look for or initiate romantic liaisons is called "snaggin'," and late night attempts to visit a person so contacted is referred to jokingly as "teepee-creeping"—though this activity should not be taken as an indication that Indian youths are any more promiscuous than their white counterparts who may use the teen dance

hall, videogame parlor, or "dragging" the main street of a large city for the same purpose. In fact, unlike white teenagers in these circumstances, the Indian young people are usually at the powwow with their parents.

Probably the most interesting peripheral activity going on during the dance, from the Indian point of view, is the stick game, a form of gambling in which two teams face each other in parallel rows and try to guess which of two marked bones a person on the opposite team has hidden in which hand. It is a complicated game (sometimes the attempt is to guess which hand holds an unmarked piece) and it goes on incessantly during some powwows with a good deal of money being bet on whether this or that team can guess properly. If the powwow is of more than one day's duration and held in a building, it often happens that the stick game will be interrupted at midnight or 1 A.M. by the closing of the building. When this occurs while a game is still in progress, an honest-looking bystander will be asked to take on the job of guarding the money which has already been wagered. It is carefully counted, tied up in a cloth bundle, and handed over to the chosen person, often a total stranger, who is ordered to be back

*Below right: A stick game tournament held at the 1987 Arlee Powwow on the Flathead Reservation in Arlee, Montana. The three men (left) constitute one team and face the opposing team across a space where the money bet on the game lies on the ground. The man in the brown jacket (middle) is hiding game pieces in his hands, and a member of the opposing team tries to guess which hand holds the unmarked piece. The hiding team is singing a song believed to have the power to confuse the other team so that they guess incorrectly. The name of the game derives from the sticks that are stuck in the ground to keep score. (FCP-OS-87-ES-16-38) Photograph by Edwin Schupman, Jr. American Folklife Center, Library of Congress*

with it the following evening in time for the game to resume.

All activities of the powwow work to foster unity, and the idea of competition among American Indians is quite different from that found among most Americans of European background, who have developed a culture in which the individual is expected to move away from home and make a success in the world by competing with others. The tribal system subscribed to by most American Indian groups is in almost total contrast to this model. Children are never left alone (a vision quest sometime between the ages of thirteen and eighteen may be the first time a young person has ever been alone except for toilet functions). Families tend to live together in limited space with many people to a room, and the tribal idea of reciprocation and sharing, which once was responsible for the very survival of people in a hunting and gathering culture, is still very much proclaimed as a virtue. Certain kinds of competition are allowed, but they are usually in the form of games, and even at that the games are often constructed so that there is no clear winner. Foot races, for example, often pair a very young person with a very old person, and both are described as running "with the sun." In other tribes certain games like stick ball or other sports are fiercely competitive, while everyday life, especially ritual life, is entirely cooperative and reciprocal.

One function of competition at the powwow is to attract good dancers. If the best dancers have a chance of winning money (which will enable them to cover the cost of their transportation), they are more likely to attend. If everyone realizes that there will be some fine dancers at the powwow, it is more likely that everyone will want to attend. The competition among Indian dancers also has the advantage of interesting the surrounding white community, who may not understand the real cultural reasons for the powwow but can appreciate the dancing, and who understand very well the notion of competition. A good competition will draw enough spectators to provide the money to pay the expenses of the powwow. Within this competition, however, there are some distinctly Indian values. The women's

dancing, for example, is judged by other Native American women who look for certain highly valued abilities that relate to Indian custom: authenticity of outfit, delicacy and style of footwork in the dance, and knowledge of the dance tune (indicated by stopping precisely when the singing stops). Similarly, in the men's traditional dancing, the dancers are judged on their knowledge of the songs, the authenticity of costume, and the forcefulness with which they portray the vision of the animal or process they are symbolizing in their dance. This encourages the cultural interests of those younger dancers who aspire to do the traditional dance steps and makes it necessary for them to learn the traditions thoroughly before they dare place themselves in competition. Thus, from the Indian point of view, it is the strengthening of tradition rather than the competition for money, trophies, or personal acclaim that is the central feature of the powwow.

In the fancy dancing, there is an even greater obligation to know the songs, for the dances are faster and the dancers are dancing so energetically that it is very difficult to stop. During the competitive fancy dancing, the drummers will try to trick the dancers by stopping suddenly in the middle of a song. The drum, however, can stop only at certain traditional places, where it is well-known that they have come to the end of a particular musical phrase. Normally, the song might go on at this point, but the drum has the option of stopping it momentarily and then starting up. When the drumming and singing stop, the best of the dancers will also be ready to stop on that same beat. Any dancer who does not stop will call attention to himself by taking another step which can be heard because of his bells. Through such trick stops as these, the less proficient dancers are eliminated from competition and the best of the fancy dancers remain. Obviously, even though part of the judgment is made on how energetically and how well they can perform the dance steps, only the ones who know the

Dance competition at the
1983 Omaha powwow.
Above: (FCP/0-CF11-5)
Photograph by Carl Fleisch-
hauer. Right: (FCP/0-
DSL5-6) Photograph by
Dorothy Sara Lee

songs and the song traditions thoroughly can possibly remain in competition until the end. Again, the stress is on the knowledge of tradition more than on competition. In addition to this, those who win the top prizes and are given money awards (which may range from $50 to $1,500) almost always share their money with the other competitors and with the drums. This redistribution of prize money is a standard feature of Indian concepts about competition and selfishness: anyone who gains riches or power by his own competitive means and does not share them with his family and friends is thought by many tribes to be a witch. Thus the tendency is not to keep money and goods but to redistribute one's own belongings as far as possible. The powwow provides a continually functional context where this may be done openly.

Very often, as concentric circles of round dancers move around the powwow pavilion, people shake hands with others who are passing in the other line, whooping loudly as they do so. One often sees the whooping or yelling directed at a non-Indian who seems to be dancing for the first time. If the person smiles and whoops back, this is greeted by whooping from all pres-

ent, but if the outsider seems embarrassed and looks away in confusion, another Indian will reach out and try to shake hands. The idea here is not to embarrass outsiders but to force them to become participants, to enclose them within the same circle. Most visitors to a powwow find this an extremely warming custom.

The concept of dancing with people as a symbol of supporting them or agreeing with them extends to a number of very important events in the lives of Indian people. For example, at some powwows there will be a special dance in which a young son who has come of age and who is about to go off to school dances around the arena with his father. On the last time around they dance down the middle until they reach the halfway point; then they turn and dance in opposite directions. At this point, both dancers and their families are often in tears, for the dance symbolizes the separation of father and son as the son moves away from the reservation area. Similarly, when middle-aged people move back to the reservation from the cities, as is often the case, they may request that the master of ceremonies at a powwow ask the people for "permission" for them to move back. Actually, they need no permission, but they are looking for the emotional and cultural support of their people. Such a couple, along with their children, may then dance alone in a round dance formation around the entire arena side by side, perhaps only four or five people alone in the entire area. Then, one by one, other members of their families, friends, and even people who have never met them before will move out and join the dancing until the entire arena is full of concentric circles. Usually at this point the family who has asked for "permission" to be reabsorbed in the tribal system is in tears because of the powerful symbolic meaning of this action.

It is also the custom when someone in the immediate family has recently died for relatives *not* to participate in the dancing of the powwow, or even to attend. But after a year has gone by, a memorial dance may be held, often combined with a powwow, in which the deceased person is praised, and his or her relatives dance in commemoration of the person. Often a younger person in the family will wear some of the traditional clothing that once belonged to the deceased, or on other occasions items belonging to the deceased will be displayed in a processional.

The powwow in its current form is an outgrowth of earlier social dances held by almost all tribes for their friends and allies.

As far back as the written histories of the Europeans in America go, there are good records of such occasions being held regularly. The difference today is that these dances are held for all tribes and not just for allies. That is, they provide for the expression of a common interest now felt by virtually all tribes who see themselves as living in a surrounded territory. Thus the intertribal connections brought about and nurtured by powwow dancing are of political as well as ethnic importance for Native Americans. Often, powwows are also the occasions for discussions by Native Americans as they develop political and legal ways in which to survive in the modern world. The stress on intertribally shared interests over tribal differences that might have existed from ancient times is expressed vividly in the powwow. Thus, even though the political interests discussed at powwows are quite modern, the use of the dance as symbolic of intertribal reciprocation and cooperation is certainly testimony to the ongoing function of older modes of thought and expression.

The powwow also provides a living context in which young people learn older patterns and experience a tremendous range of expressions based on worldview assumptions that remain important to Indian people. In addition, the process takes place in concert with the whole family and tribe; the model provided at a powwow is an idealized model of cultural and ethnic stability that for many American Indians is one of the few ways to combat the instability, erosion, and conflict brought about in their cultural lives by the European invasion.

During the powwow there is a conscious nurturing and intensification of generally shared tribal attitudes that exist outside language and ritual, as well as a deference to the cultural differences which still exist among the various tribes. Such ideas as circularity, time as an outgrowth of the event (rather than vice versa), models of reciprocation, competition within culturally acceptable and meaningful contexts (a way of controlling a white idea that otherwise causes trouble), the importance of the family as a unit, all are seen by Native Americans as promoting stability, while the absence of these factors is seen as erosive and corrosive to Native American culture. The powwow, with all of its dancing patterns and reciprocal modes of operation, provides a living model of tribal attitudes; it can be planned and integrated into the everyday lives of Indian people without endangering their livelihoods or their survival in a sometimes hazardous and aggressive world.

There is of course a certain amount of nostalgia for an older way of life, and the widespread use of the tipi at the larger outdoor encampments is one way of recapturing this older way. But Indians acknowledge today that the old way has indeed changed forever and that to survive they must now combine aspects of their older customs with realities of the world in which they live. No one believes, in other words, that the Europeans will move back to Europe and the Indians back to tipis. Nonetheless, no one believes that an Indian needs to stop being an Indian in order to live in his own country. Thus, while most Indians take jobs when they can in the American economy, and most have adopted generally American styles of clothing for everyday life, what they have done on the other hand is to intensify and solidify the occasions on which they can celebrate the continued existence of Indian ways of life at home. Since taking a job or going to school often necessitates leaving one's family, thus setting up an instability in the tribal system, the powwow functions as a way of bringing people symbolically back together for the encouragement and nurturing of their ethnic lives and their continued existence as a people. In this sense, the new way of life does not entirely replace the old; the old survives by adapting and intensifying. The powwow is one dynamic example of how ethnic selection and intensification function to preserve cultural values even under the most trying circumstances. Clearly, the "Vanishing Americans" of popular belief have not vanished; they're still dancing.

# Celebration

## Native Events in Eastern Canada

BY MICHAEL SAM CRONK,
with BEVERLEY CAVANAGH
and FRANZISKA VON ROSEN

Every summer Native people come together at regional powwows and festivals
to express their cultural heritage through
music and dance. These events are opportunities to socialize and to celebrate with
other Native nations, and for non-Native
audiences to share this experience. Three of
the larger regional events are the Grand
River "Champion of Champions" powwow
in southern Ontario; the Micmac summer
games in New Brunswick and Nova Scotia;
and the Innu Nikamu festival in northern
Quebec. Each is a unique annual gathering
featuring Native music and dance, bringing
people together from many nations.

At these events, two central ideas
emerge: the continued importance of music
and dance for Native cultural expression,
and the diversity as well as unity of Native
traditions throughout this region. The continuity and innovation of the events reflect
the vitality of these traditions.

*Traditional Micmac*
*ji'kmaqn (slapstick).*
*Photograph by M. S. Cronk*

Since the early 1970s, competition powwows have become increasingly popular throughout central and western Canada and the United States. Almost every weekend from late March through September, dancers and drummers from across North America travel to Native reserves, urban centers, and university campuses to take part in local and regional powwows. Each year more get-togethers are added to the powwow circuits.

Historically the word *powwow* has been used in different ways; its meaning still varies across eastern Canada. Possibly, it originated among New England Algonquian tribes, where a "powwow" was a "man of power" or "shaman." In Ontario during the nineteenth century, the word was used to describe events ranging from religious processions blending Roman Catholic and Native traditions to special performances of music and dance for Native and non-Native audiences.[1] Currently, in Quebec and the Maritimes, powwows may com-

*Right: Traditional dancer at the Champion of Champions Powwow at the Six Nations reserve in southern Ontario, July 1986. In the background is the dance arbor. Photograph by M. S. Cronk*

*Far right: Getting ready for the Champion of Champions Powwow, July 1986. Photograph by M. S. Cronk*

"Great Law," codes structuring a complex system of religious, political, and social practices. The powwow developed out of earlier dance shows and rodeos sponsored during the summer by the Six Nations singing societies, which are social "mutual aid" organizations.[3]

Powwows are not part of traditional Iroquoian culture, though in some ways they complement Longhouse beliefs; their focal elements, music and dance, celebrate the physical and spiritual worlds around us in ways comparable with Iroquoian social music. But the introduction of powwows to Iroquoian communities has created tension among more conservative Longhouse people, since the events involve competitions for prizes. Longhouse beliefs stress that the ability to sing and dance is "a gift from the Creator," to be used for the benefit of the community rather than for personal gain. But many singers and dancers say that winning the competitions is secondary; the success of a powwow is really determined by the "good feeling" generated through friendship, respect, pride in one's self, and pride in "being Indian." People join together to celebrate their collective heritage, creating unity among nations rather than weakening traditional Iroquoian beliefs.

The powwow is held at Chiefswood Park by the Grand River during the last weekend of July. Weeks in advance, the powwow committee prepares the grounds. A dance arbor is set up toward the center of the clearing, sheltering drums and sound equipment. Dancers compete in the area directly surrounding the arbor, roped off from the audience. Food and craft booths line the field.

bine music and dance, games, feasts, and fireworks.

Contemporary competition powwows in Ontario are a blend of dancing, singing, and drumming. They include sports events, community and cultural displays, and food and craft booths; but at the center of the gathering is the large social drum, considered by many as the heartbeat of the *Anisinabek* nations, or "first people" of North America.[2] Every participant, every activity seems to revolve around and move to the sound of these "big drums."

The Champion of Champions powwow originated in 1979, rapidly becoming a favorite among powwow singers and dancers. It is hosted by members of the Six Nations Reserve, an Iroquoian community near Brantford, Ontario. There are approximately seven thousand band members at Six Nations; most follow either Christian or traditional Longhouse Iroquoian beliefs, based on the *Gai'wiio* (or "Good Message" of Seneca prophet Handsome Lake) and the

P eople arrive early that weekend to set up their booths, get ready for the competitions, or find a good seat near the arbor. The powwow officially begins around noon, with a ceremony raising both Canadian and American flags and the Grand Entry parade; all dancers take part in this procession, led by veterans from Six Nations. Next, a special flag dance honors all Native veterans. Then, a community elder from Six

Nations says the *Ganohonyon,* or Iroquoian "Thanksgiving Address," a formal speech thanking the Creator for all those things provided to us.[4] After welcoming speeches by the powwow committee, the afternoon continues with a mixture of competitions and intertribal dances, in which the audience sometimes participates. Unlike a number of powwows organized by Algonquian communities, there are no sunrise ceremonies or pipe ceremonies at Grand River, since these are not part of Iroquoian traditions.

At powwows, people generally dance in a clockwise circle, the direction that the sun follows. Among many Algonquian nations, this is the direction that all living things are believed to travel. This contrasts, however, with Iroquoian beliefs; at Longhouse "socials," people dance in a counterclockwise circuit, which for them is the direction of life. The direction you move depends on the kind and context of the dance itself.

Drummers, dancers, and their families from many nations join in at Grand River; some come from Alberta and the western provinces, others from North Dakota, Arizona, and Oklahoma. Their dance outfits and singing and dance styles reflect a wide range of traditions. For example, the men's traditional dance* outfits vary considerably. All wear moccasins, buckskin or cloth leggings, and breechcloths, but there is much innovation and individuality, particularly in the feather headdresses or hair roaches they wear, the ribbons, beads, or quillwork decorating their outfits, and the large feather bustles.[5] Some Iroquoian dancers combine traditional *Houdenosaunee*[6] and powwow outfit styles, wearing a *gustoweh* (Iroquoian headdress) rather than Plains style hair roaches, or deer dewclaw garters instead of the more common bell garters around their legs.

Some traditional dancers are thought to borrow from the actions of birds and animals. As they move, they are transformed, taking on the characteristics of the animals. Dancing is a way of expressing and af-

*Throughout this article the dances men's traditional, women's traditional, men's fancy, and women's fancy shawl refer to specialized powwow dance genres.

firming their strong connection with the natural and spiritual worlds.

There are many other dance categories at a powwow, each distinguished by costume and step. Men fancy dancers wear bright, multicolored outfits, with two bustles at the back and color-coordinated beadwork, leggings, hair roaches, and moccasins. Their innovative dancing style is characterized by energetic splits, spins, and jumps, all in time with the drumbeat.

Women traditional dancers usually wear cloth or buckskin outfits, beaded moccasins, belts, hair ornaments, and necklaces. They often carry feather fans and brightly colored shawls, decorated with fringes, beadwork, and embroidered or quilted designs. Their dancing is comparatively restrained; usually, their feet barely leave the ground, which physically expresses a personal connection to the earth itself. Women fancy-shawl dancers often wear brightly colored dresses, shawls, and moccasins elaborately decorated with beads and sequins. Like the men fancy dancers, their dancing style is faster and more energetic. In the summer of 1987, a women's jingle dress competition was added. In this tradition, the women's dresses are decorated with rows of small metal cones (or "jingles"), which create a beautiful sound as they move.

Competitions last from noon until late evening. Dancers are judged primarily on their poise, stamina, constant movement, and respect for the drum and for each other. They must dance in time with the drumbeat, stopping exactly when the song ends, and must withdraw from the competition if they drop part of their outfit. It takes considerable experience and skill to become a champion powwow dancer.

Drums (the term refers both to the instrument and the group) are also judged on their professionalism, repertoire, performance ability, and respect for the drum. Drummers at these events are always male, although sometimes women singers join them, standing behind the men as they sing. The instruments may be either handmade or commercially produced bass drums. The former consist of round wooden frames varying in height and diameter according to each drum maker; there are usually two drum heads (or membranes), often made from cowhide, which are lashed to the frame. Drums may be suspended from a four-cornered drum stand, or they may rest on a blanket placed on the ground. Drum frames, heads, and stands are often decorated with a group's name or other designs of considerable symbolic importance.[7]

There are different styles of powwow singing. Groups from Ontario often perform in a Northern Plains style, characterized by a high, tense, heavily pulsated voice. The lead singer begins, with other drummers taking up and extending the song, usually repeating it four times through (though this varies among different groups). During the last repeat, the steady rhythm of the drum becomes faster and louder, and the dancing more intense.

Several Iroquoian drums compete at this and other powwows. Many of these groups are fairly new, forming within the last four years. Most Iroquoian drummers are Longhouse people. They retain their traditional beliefs, language and culture, but they also enjoy getting together and singing powwow songs. Although powwows are not part of Iroquoian traditions, these singers clearly express their respect for the "big drum," and for the event itself.

Musically, their singing styles are similar to non-Iroquoian groups, yet these groups are unique in several ways. Iroquoian singers almost exclusively use commercially made drums, adapted and decorated with Iroquoian designs (such as wampum belts, or the "tree of peace"). Additionally, few of these groups create their own powwow songs, developing their repertoire instead from commercially released tapes or recordings from other powwows. The more powwows you attend, the easier it becomes to identify where participants are from, by their singing styles, outfits, dance steps, or the drums they use.

On Saturday night, after competitions end, Iroquoian singers (both men and women) get together and socialize; not only the drummers, but dancers, judges, members of the audience join in—everyone who knows Iroquois social dances. Significantly, this music is not used for competition at this powwow, though Iroquois dance competitions have been introduced in New York State.

The Iroquoian social dances vary considerably from powwow songs. They are performed at a lower pitch, with a more relaxed vocal style (less of the throbbing or pulsating sound that characterizes powwow music). The lead singer plays a water drum, a small wooden or plastic keg with a single leather head. The drum contains a small amount of water, which tunes the head and helps create a loud ringing sound. (If a water drum is not available, however, some singers have used the "big drum" at these events.) Other singers play cow horn rattles, made from a section of horn filled with pebbles or shot. There are thirty or

*Singers from the Treaty of 1794 (Iroquoian) drum group perform at Dorseyville, Pennsylvania, September 1986. Photograph by M. S. Cronk*

more social dance sets, each with a distinctive melody and step. Some, like the *eskanye,* or "women's shuffle dance," are traditionally Iroquoian; others, like the Rabbit or Round dances, have been borrowed and adapted from western nations.

Competitions end Sunday evening with an awards presentation, when cash prizes and trophies are presented. The powwow concludes with a final victory dance, honoring all contest winners.

Powwows have often been described as pan-Indian events, suggesting that Native music and traditions are blended almost inseparably into one, unified pan-Indian culture. Although the Champion of Champions powwow is an integrative force, it is clearly more appropriate to describe it as an intertribal (rather than pan-Indian) gathering. Of course each powwow is different from every other, influenced by different organizers, participants, and settings. The Champion of Champions powwow is in turn shaped by Longhouse Iroquoian traditions—through, for example, the *Gano-honyon,* Iroquois social dancing, and the omission of pipe and sunrise ceremonies. This powwow does not submerge regional traditions and values; instead, it is a vehicle that allows different nations to express a common bond as *Ongwehonwe,* or "real people/first people" of North America.

The search for a Native/Micmac/Maliseet identity has taken many forms in the Maritimes. Unlike the Iroquois and Ojibwe nations from Ontario, the Wabanaki nation (including the Micmacs, Maliseets, Penobscots, and Passamaquoddy) has lost many of its traditional cultural teachings, particularly with regard to ceremonies, rituals, songs, and dances.

The search for identity has become, for the most part, an individual quest. For some who call themselves traditionalists, this has meant learning from Native elders in Alberta, North and South Dakota, and elsewhere, and bringing back diverse teachings about the "big drum," pipe ceremonies, and the sweat lodge. For others, particularly the Maliseets, it has meant searching in Maine and along the eastern seaboard for elders who still remember Wabanaki songs and dances. Other groups, including the dance troupes, search within their own communities for the few remaining elders who have some memory of traditional Micmac songs and dances.

Powwows (whether traditional or competition) are not part of Native cultural expression in the Maritime provinces. Occasionally, an event (or part of an event) is called a powwow, but this usually refers more to the fact that at some point, the "big drum" will be played. Recently, some of the traditional drummers have considered organizing a "real" powwow in the Maritimes, but to date this has not happened.

Instead, in the east, the most popular forum for the expression of Native identity is the annual round of summer games and gatherings. Traditional gatherings are held seasonally, most popularly in the spring and fall. The summer games, held annually since 1972, are usually held in July, because in August many Micmacs and Maliseets take part in the annual blueberry harvest in Maine.

The summer games provide a way to bring Christians and traditionalists together for a few days of fun and competition. In Nova Scotia and New Brunswick, reserves take turns hosting the games. Preparations such as advertising, fund raising, and grounds maintenance begin a year in advance. Until recently, the main emphasis at these games has been athletic competitions. This is gradually changing, however, as more cultural events such as "eel skinning," "tea boiling," Micmac dance competitions, and *waltes* games (a traditional social gambling game) are included in the program.[8]

Activities at the summer games in Cambridge, Nova Scotia, in 1986 were divided into three categories: sports events, with softball heading the list; social events such as bingo, a "Princess pageant," and a concert and dance; and the "o'l pasn games," including Micmac dance competitions, chanting, *waltes* games, a sweat lodge, pipe ceremonies, and an outdoor mass in the "cultural village" (a small area set aside for these games on the reserve, designated as drug and alcohol free).

A drum, the Birch Creek Singers (traditionalists following western Native teachings), and a dance group, the Micmac Dancers (Christians with a Micmac social dance repertoire), performed together in the opening and closing ceremonies in the cultural village. Teepees were set up in the area, and the drummers and their families stayed there. Although the "big drum" is not part of the Wabanaki tradition, it plays a part in the current cultural revival and is used when singing intertribal as well as Wabanaki songs. At the Cambridge games, the singers performed Micmac songs during the official ceremonies, but switched mainly to "intertribals" as well as a few Iroquoian social dances for informal events.

The song repertoire of the Birch Creek Singers reflects the different influences that have helped to shape the individual singer's concepts of Native/Micmac identity. The current group (all male) was formed in 1985. Previously, a former lead singer preferred Wabanaki songs. The current lead singer prefers western style powwow songs (though he was born in Cape Breton, Nova Scotia, and his father knew Micmac songs). Now, whenever the group is without their lead singer, they perform mainly Wabanaki songs—possibly, as the lead singer suggests, because they have difficulty singing the high-pitched powwow songs. Whatever the reason, the drum's repertoire is certainly not limited to pan-Indian songs.

In the east, as in Ontario, women singers do not usually sit at the "big drum." They occasionally stand behind the drummers and sing with them. With regard to the dance troupes, however, it is the women who are usually the drummers, singers, and dancers. These women have learned the traditional songs and dances from Micmac elders and are now reintegrating this music into their communities through performances at schools, conferences, and the summer games. The Micmac dancers who performed in Cambridge are a group of women and children from Eskasoni Reserve, Nova Scotia.[9] The women make the traditional Micmac costumes and teach children the dances.

At the Cambridge summer games, the opening welcome dance was performed by both drummers and the dance group. Dancers moved clockwise around the "big drum," using a soft toe-heel step (three steps forward and two back). Other dances included the game dance, the feather dance, and the Native dance (also called the Micmac dance). The latter is a favorite among the dancers; it has a fast tempo and an energetic dance step—with two steps forward and one back, first with the right foot, and then with the left. Micmac social dances performed during the opening ceremonies have a certain similarity to Iroquoian social songs, both in the general dance step and in the vocal style.[10]

The two instruments usually played by the dance groups are the *ji'kmaqn* (a type of slapstick made of pounded ash) and a double-headed frame drum; both are made locally. Although one or two drum makers are always identified, other people do make their own, handing them down from one family member to another. The "big drum"

used by drums such as the Birch Creek Singers is often made by the singers themselves, sometimes with the aid of drum makers from other nations (such as the Ojibwe). Many of the horn rattles used by both drummers and dancers are of Iroquoian origin.

The response of the audience (which for the most part was Native) to both drummers and dancers was warm and enthusiastic. Yet when invited to join in and dance around the drum, very few people responded. At gatherings where mainly traditionalists take part, most people do join in. But here at the games, where the "big drum" and the dance troupes are relatively new additions, the majority of people prefer to stand back and listen.

The broad and constantly changing spectrum of events that shape the summer games in this region reveals the struggle and tensions, as well as the strength and commonality, that define the search for Native identity among these people. Despite the diversity of contemporary beliefs and ways, they are able to come together for enjoyment, friendship, and competition. In bringing together eastern and western Native song and dance styles, Christian and Native ceremonies, Native and non-Native participants, these games contribute to a sense of community and mutual respect that is at the heart of Native teachings.

*Waltes game being played at the 1987 summer games. Photograph by Franziska von Rosen*

Dance performance at La
Fête de la famille abenakise, Quebec 1986. Photo-
graph by B. A. Cavanagh

In Quebec and Labrador, Indian identity
is again defined and presented differently at
intertribal events. For the Naskapi, Montagnais, Eastern Cree, and Attikamek nations, identity is virtually inseparable from
one's Native language. People often speak
proudly about the fact that in these areas
virtually everyone, young and old, is fluent
in his or her own tongue; many also speak
French. The Huron community at Lorette-
ville, Quebec, or the western Abenaki of
Odanak, on the other hand, are more similar to the Micmac, since many of their cultural traditions (including language) were
lost and are now being retaught with the assistance of elders and community-run institutions such as museums.

In most Quebec and Labrador communities, the majority of people are Roman
Catholic. However, the adaptation of
Christian traditions and, in the case of the
Montagnais, the distinctiveness of their language ensures that this borrowing of a European religion is considered to be a part of
their Indian identity. Few people express
any sense of conflict between Christian and
indigenous religious traditions; for example, a mass is consistently scheduled at
intertribal gatherings. So when people from
various nations in Quebec and Labrador
meet at intertribal events, they celebrate
not only their common heritage as Native
people but also the richness and variety of
their traditions. To some extent, this is like

the Grand River powwow or Micmac summer games, where many traditions are enjoyed. Unlike the powwow, however, many new songs (especially within the Montagnais community) are created in a variety of popular styles.

Traditional songs from this area are hard to describe as "artifacts," because the singer/drummer responds to the situation at hand, performing slightly differently on each occasion.[11] One can therefore speak about different styles of singing more easily than different styles of songs. Each region has a distinctive voice, a unique style of *nikuman* (song), however, and these are easily recognized by those who know the tradition. Cree singers, for example, speak of a high and low section within the song, whereas Montagnais *nikumana* sometimes move within a low register. It takes a lot of listening to begin to observe the subtle differences between each community's singing style.

One singer/organizer of the Innu Nikamu festival expressed his appreciation for these differences, saying:

Each musician has his own talent to make worth something. It doesn't matter where he comes from or what style of music he does. . . . Each musician has his music for himself, no matter if he sings the song of someone else. I think that there is a personality in each musician, in each music. Several musicians can do the same song but it is different each time.

Perhaps the emphasis on individual song style is like the emphasis on distinctive costumes or dance moves at a powwow. On the other hand, all the musical styles in the widespread Montagnais/Naskapi/Eastern Cree dialects share certain features. For example, both traditional and contemporary Montagnais folksongs are regarded as truly Montagnais, because the rhythm and meaning of the texts for both styles are distinctively Montagnais. As Florant "Ty Ty" Vollant, one of the most popular singers in Maliotenam, said:

[The difference in the music] . . . it is the language. The language is very strong. There is also an uncertain rhythm in the music known here . . . the native element is the rhythm. And also the message of the artists in their songs. I think that is also different.

As in Ontario and the Maritimes, intertribal events are called by many names. The word *powwow* is used, though less frequently than in Ontario and areas further west. In Quebec, it refers to a multifaceted community event, unlike those dance competitions featuring the "big drum."[12] Some celebrations (or parts of celebrations) are also called by the Algonquian term *mokushan*. While this traditionally refers to a sacred ritual associated with caribou hunting, the spiritual connotations are not overt at contemporary gatherings.

French names such as *fête* are sometimes considered appropriate. With some exceptions, a *fête* usually has a strong association with Christian celebrations; hence the "Fête Montagnaise" at Betsiamites, Quebec, coincides with the Feast of the Assumption on August 15. Finally, the English name "gathering" has been used since 1985 in Labrador; it refers to a week-long retreat "in the country" where "town-dwellers" may learn traditional Native ways from their elders and where Catholic services coexist with traditional events such as drum dancing.

For Native events in Quebec, then, as with the summer games and the Grand River powwow, the term *pan-Indian* is not appropriate. Not only do intertribal events contain widely different types of music, but different events have their own distinctive profile.

When a group at Sept Iles/Maliotenam decided to organize a major festival in 1985, they selected a Montagnais name, in this case one of their own creation: "Innu Nikamu" (The Indian Sings). In many ways Innu Nikamu is the most experimental event among Native communities in Quebec, incorporating the broadest range of traditions of all the intercommunity and intertribal gatherings.

This four-day festival, held in early August, brings together several thousand Native people (estimates ranged from three to ten thousand in 1986), largely from Quebec and Labrador. To an outsider, it appears to borrow elements of the American folk festival, rock concert, and Christian holiday. The event is seen primarily as a way of drawing people together, although it is not without some controversial aspects. Some people dislike its structured schedule, claiming that it is organized "with the mentality of whites."

The site for the festival is a large open field opposite one of the two schools in Maliotenam. A stage, facing east, is erected for the festival's duration; it is raised about six feet above the ground, and hence is a distinctly separate area. The performers and audience are set apart to a large extent, as they are at a concert. Nevertheless, listeners sometimes form dance circles immediately below the stage or to one side of it, dancing to both traditional and contemporary singer/drummers. The only traditional element of the stage area is the central ridgepole, at right angles to the audience, from which the *teueikan* (a single-membrane frame drum)

is suspended for Montagnais traditional performances.

Four large fires (to the north, south, east, and west of the site) are prepared in advance of each evening concert and lit around dusk. In August 1986 concerts lasted from 6 P.M. until midnight. They began with a traditional performance—either one or more *teueikan* players, or an unaccompanied Abenaki singer—which served as a gesture of respect for the elders, and as a kind of opening prayer. People danced spontaneously during the drum performances; moving in the customary counterclockwise circle, both men and women did the *makusham* step (two small steps in a ♪♪ rhythm, with a knee bend on each ♪). People sometimes say that this step recreates the tracks that one sees on the hunt. Once again, as at the powwows, the dancers express a "transformation," or link with animals.

Each concert served a slightly different purpose. Although all the evening programs appeared to encompass several types of music, the feeling at each performance was different. At the first concert, people celebrated musicians from their midst; at others, they welcomed those from other communities. The third performance (which

*Craft demonstration at La Fête de la famille abenakise, Quebec 1986. Photograph by B. A. Cavanagh*

*Réal Vollant, on guitar, and his "folk" group performing at the Innu Nikamu festival, Maliotenam, Quebec, August 1986. Photograph by B. A. Cavanagh*

received the greatest hype as "la crème de la crème") featured Native recording artists from Ottawa, Montreal, and other large cities. Slicker orchestral arrangements and a greater array of mainstream pop idioms characterized much of the program. To a large extent, however, the energy of the previous concerts was not regained, perhaps because, as one singer said, "the heart is with the people who have contact with the population."

In addition to evening concerts, daytime programs were organized for the weekend, including games, presentations of traditional legends, and children's songs from different parts of the world. On Sunday an outdoor mass was held in the morning,

while the afternoon was left open for unscheduled performances.

The traditional drum, the *teueikan*, was a visible symbol for the event. It figured prominently in the festival logo, which consisted of a fire-rimmed drum with a guitar overlaid, the latter merging with the body of a goose. A large, red-rimmed *teueikan* was used by traditional drummers Jean-Baptiste Jean-Pierre (Uashat) and Joseph McKenzie (Schefferville). Two drum rhythms are readily apparent in their music; the first, a sort of tremolo accompanying a narrow-ranged song; the second, a dance rhythm that could be notated as ♫. Characteristic of the drum's sound is the buzz of a pair of snares which intersect the circle of the drum head at right angles. These snares embody the voices heard in one's dreams.

The texts of these traditional songs are understood by those meant to know their message. For others, the words are obscured by the snare's buzz, as well as by extra syllables (or vocables) added by the singer. On the other hand, virtually everybody knows the words to contemporary songs, which often feature distinctive, "strong" Montagnais messages. These are deeply meaningful to many people; some honor the past (as in the title song of Phillippe McKenzie's popular album "Mistashipu"—Great River), while others celebrate the Innu's connectedness to family, friends, and the land.

Additionally, the musical styles of contemporary songs have features which represent continuity with older traditions. Although these songs are often accompanied by the guitar, "folk singers" at Maliotenam sometimes use the *teueikan*, but with the snares removed. The characteristic buzz is not entirely relinquished, though, since maracas are often added to ensembles to duplicate that sound; some drummers use a maraca as a drum-beater, while others shake the rattle in accompaniment. Finally, the distinctive uncertain or unpredictable rhythm of this music (heterometric, in musicological terms) is also considered uniquely Indian. Vocal patterns are repeated in elusive, asymmetrical groups, sometimes countering the accompanying rhythm of the percussive instruments.

But generalizations about these musical styles are dangerous since, as Vollant says, "Each musician has his own talent to make worth something. It doesn't matter what genre of music he does." So we return to the notion of this festival celebrating a richness and diversity of tradition, while at the same time consolidating support for Native music in Quebec.

These three different events—the Champion of Champions powwow, the summer games, and the Innu Nikamu festival—all provide opportunities for shared Native expression, highlighting interactions among communities.

Understanding the complexity of the interactions is important. At these gatherings there are no simple, rigid boundaries separating Native communities and cultures. Although distinct musics and musical styles exist, many social music traditions borrow selectively from one another, adapting styles and forms to suit their needs and aesthetics. Musicians may perform and create music characteristic of other communities or nations. Distinctions among music and dance styles, dance outfits, or instrumentation may at times seem to blur, yet individual or tribal identities are not relinquished.

At these intertribal events, it is not essential that the music (or even the event itself) be entirely traditional to the region; the songs and dances are perhaps the raw material to which performers or communities apply their own values and traditions, which in turn shape these gatherings. In light of this, concepts of pan-Indianism or acculturation often seem too simplistic and generalized to have any real meaning when discussing contemporary Native realities in eastern Canada.

At another level, a common element of Native cultural identity is expressed throughout the region: the sense of connectedness between people and the natural environment. Singers and dancers in these communities often acknowledge their relationship with the environment as fundamental to their economic and physical survival, to their cultural and spiritual ways of life. It is in fact basic to their integrity as a people. Through songs and dances, people affirm their relationship to this land, to the animals, birds, and water, to the earth itself.

At these events, social music and dance both reflect and create interactions—among individuals and communities, among people and the physical and spiritual worlds around them. Connections renewed through the gatherings are fundamental expressions of cultural identity. Music and dance are not simply symbols of one's heritage—they are active ways of living it, showing how individuals and nations fit in with the rest of the world.

# NOTES

The authors attended the events described above as members of SPINC (Sound Producing Instruments in Native Communities), a cultural research project based at Queen's University at Kingston, Ontario, Canada. They would like to thank the Social Science and Humanities Research Council of Canada for funding the SPINC project.

1. Such events are identified as "powwows" in photographs in the Public Archives of Ontario (Toronto) collection. For example, in photographs dating from 1899, from Rainy River, Ontario (#10399–19), the powwow is a presentation by a single drum and costumed dancers for a Native and non-Native audience.

2. *Anisinabek* is an Ojibwe (Algonquian) word referring to the Native people or "first people" of North America; the corresponding Iroquoian word is *ongwehonwe*, or "real people/first people."

3. Most Iroquoian communities have one or more singing societies that meet regularly to sing new *eskanye* (women's shuffle dance), the only Iroquois social dance set for which new songs are regularly created. Primarily, these groups organized to raise money or otherwise to help those in need. Cronk is currently working with a number of singers from these societies.

4. An excellent analysis of the "Thanksgiving Address" is found in M. K. Foster's *From the Earth to Beyond the Sky: An Ethnographic Approach to Four Longhouse Iroquois Speech Events* (Ottawa: National Museums of Canada, 1974), Mercury series no. 20.

5. Bustles are made from eagle wings, feathers, and sometimes beadwork, constructed in a "circular or U-shaped configuration." They are attached by a belt or strap around the dancer's waist and worn at the mid-back level. *See also 200 Years in the Making: Commemorative Program* (Ohsweken: Grand River Powwow Committee, 1984).

6. *Haudenosaunee* is an Iroquoian word meaning "People of the Longhouse"; it is used frequently among these communities instead of the more recent term *Iroquois*.

7. One common design is a circle and cross motif, visible on many drums. This single image has multiple layers of meaning, the most obvious referring to the cycle of life, the dance cycle, the earth, moon and sun, the medicine hoop, the four directions, and the four seasons.

8. At the 1986 summer games at Indian Island, New Brunswick, the chief announced that the "cultural" aspects of the games were becoming so popular among Native people that in the future, Indian Island would host annual "Cultural Games."

9. Occasionally, men dance with this group, but at these games, one woman chanted and drummed, leading the dancers, while four girls and two boys (aged ca. eight to fourteen) performed the dances.

10. Mohawk singers from Kahnawake, Quebec, often go to Micmac/Maliseet gatherings, where Iroquois social dances such as the Stomp and Rabbit dances are particular favorites. In fact, some Micmacs joke that the Mohawks "stole their songs."

11. For example, at the Innu Nikamu festival in 1986, one drummer sang for only a few minutes at the first evening concert, but felt it appropriate to sing for a longer time at the next performance.

12. In 1986 at Pointe Bleue, Quebec, a "powwow" featured foot races, canoe races and rifle firing competitions, as well as softball and horseshoe tournaments. Cultural events included marionette shows, a theater troupe, performances by Montagnais *chansonniers,* and a *spectâcle* by local musicians "Jerry and Jo Anne." Quebec events usually feature special activities for children, including races or treasure hunts.

# Reverend C.L. Franklin

## Black American Preacher-Poet

BY JEFF TODD TITON

In Detroit's New Bethel Baptist Church on Mother's Day evening in 1977 the air is palpably hot, pushed about by women waving paper fans to clear a breathing space.[1] I am standing in an aisle, making a documentary videotape. At the pulpit, the Reverend C. L. Franklin, the most celebrated black Baptist preacher of his generation and father of the "queen of soul music," Aretha Franklin, is preaching. For twenty minutes the congregation has listened to their pastor's extemporaneous message on Mary at the Cross, and now they are anxious for "the sweet part," that hypnotic, half-chanted and half-sung closing section when his message will move them to ecstasy.

Franklin's tone shifts; he begins to draw out the last syllables of certain words. The range of his spoken intonation compresses nearly to a monotone; then, gradually, it expands as he starts to chant, telling the

*Rev. C. L. Franklin, New Bethel Baptist Church, Detroit, Michigan, May 28, 1977. Photograph by Jeff Todd Titon*

story of a mother whose son was condemned to die. On the morning the son was to be hanged, the mother climbed into the belfry and held the bell clapper, for she knew an old

> tradition
> that went on and obtained
> in that country:
> before they hanged
> anybody
> they had to ring the bell.

Cries from the congregation punctuate the ends of Franklin's phrases and encourage him to continue: "That's right," "Preach, Reverend," "Tell the truth." The lines become more regular in length. He establishes a melody, its tonic reinforced by the congregation's intoned response on the tonic pitch. The pace accelerates. Reverend Franklin chants about the mother in the bell tower:

> And as they pulled the bell,
> the bell swung over
>        from one side to another.
> O Lord.
>    She fell
>    against the iron wall
>        of that big bell.
>    O Lord.
>    She was bruised,
>    she was bleeding,
>    but she held on
>        to the bell clapper,
> oh yes she did.
> Yes.
>    And after awhile,
>        they gave up.
>    After awhile
>    they said, "Since the bell won't ring,
>        we can't execute him."

The mother's fate now becomes the pastor's concern, and the congregation responds ever more loudly and forcefully. As with one voice, almost drawing the sermon out of him, the congregation cries out, the pace quickens again and the sermon comes to a singing climax:

> O Lord.
>    By that time
>    she fell down
>        upon the ground
>        under the bell clapper,

> with blood
> running from her nose,
> from her eyes
>        and from her shoulders.
> O Lord.
>    She said, "Well, son
>    I know you meant good.
>    You are my child.
>    Go on.
>    Don't worry.
>    Don't worry
>    about me.
>    I'm all right."

New Bethel is shouting in ecstasy, its people "falling out" (fainting) in the Spirit, in trance. Dancing across the pulpit, dodging a handkerchief that someone has thrown, in the midst of the deafening tumult, Franklin concludes in a burst of inspiration:

> Did you know
> that Jesus,
>    Jesus
> held the bell clapper
> of time and eternity
>        in his hands?
> Oh well,
> ohh,
> yes!

Nurses in the congregation minister to those who have fainted with excitement. Pastor Franklin winds down and extends the Invitation to people to come forward to join the church; the Lord has worked his will this morning.

Black American chanted preaching in the Protestant tradition emerged before Emancipation among the slave "exhorters" who sermonized to their fellow slaves in a spontaneous, chanted discourse. Extemporaneous prayers were chanted as well. Today the practices continue among some Baptist and Pentecostal congregations. Besides their importance in the history of black American religious practice, chanted black sermons form a literature of considerable merit. In *A Journey in the Back Country*, written shortly before the Civil War, Frederick Law Olmsted described a New Orleans slave preacher's sermon: "Much of the language was highly metaphorical; the figures long, strange, and complicated, yet sometimes, however, strangely beautiful."[2] Indeed, black American writers, including James Weldon Johnson and Zora Neale Hurston, have periodically set chanted sermons as poetry and argued strenuously in behalf of their literary value, but their argument has fallen on deaf ears. Some of the standard American literature anthologies include black spirituals and secular songs but not black sermons. This is unfortunate, for the chanted black sermon is a vigorous, living form and tradition, and authentic texts are available dating back to antebellum times. In fact, folklorists and journalists such as John and Alan Lomax and John Henry Faulk collected and recorded sermons in the 1930s and 1940s, while commercial recordings of sermons, sold in the black communities, have been available since the 1920s. Sales of the Reverend J. M. Gates's sermon records in the 1920s were exceeded in the black "race" record market only by Bessie Smith's blues records, and among black people old enough to remember his records, Reverend Gates's name is well-known. Long-playing albums, introduced in the early 1950s, allowed sermons recorded on location to be presented in their entirety. Reverend Franklin pioneered in this field; for more than thirty years, his recorded sermons have been marketed in the black communities, and more of his sermon albums have been sold than any other preacher's. One minister I interviewed in Atlanta in 1975 said he thought every black Baptist preacher from fifteen to fifty had been influenced by Franklin's preaching records.

The origin of the black American chanted sermon is hard to pinpoint. The facts are that travelers reported African and African-derived religious practices among black slaves throughout the New World, including dance, trance, spirit possession, and the ring shout; and they reported chanted sermons and prayers (in English) in the American South. In *The Art of the American Folk Preacher,* Bruce Rosenberg hypothesized that the chanted sermon was first an Anglo-American phenomenon, deriving from the emotional intonation of the exhortations of Baptist and Methodist preachers during the Second Great Awakening, that is, in the early nineteenth century. "White preachers passed the chanted sermon along to their Negro brethren" in the border states of the South, Rosenberg suggested, citing as evidence the existence today of the chanted sermon tradition among whites in eastern Kentucky, a tradition they say is at least as old as their grandparents.[3] Gerald Davis, on the other hand, contends that the "African-American sermon style, if not theology . . . has historic precedent in the affective religious and secular narrative systems of several . . . African groups."[4] Davis thinks it is more likely that the ancestors of the whites in eastern Kentucky who chant their sermons learned the practice from black Americans, who in chanting their sermons were extending an African performance medium to America. The controversy should not obscure the fact that the black chanted sermon has had a history of development since Emancipation, that not all black preachers chant today, and that among those who do there is considerable variation in the amount and type of chanting. Moreover, one of the most important influences on the development of black Christian preaching was the interchange resulting from travel among blacks within the New World and to and from Africa, both before and after Emancipation. For example, James A. Aggrey (1875–1927), a black, African-born, Christian missionary with a master's degree from Columbia University, toured the United States, lecturing and preaching as an apostle of "cooperation" between white and black. His biographer noted Aggrey's great skill with metaphor, parable, and oratory in general, and attributed it to his African background.[5] Aggrey's most famous sermon was "The Eagle Stirreth Her Nest," and its story about the farmer who raised an eagle among his chickens remains in oral tradition in black American sermons today; Reverend Franklin has a stirring version of it on Chess Records 21. Franklin himself, of course, has had a major influence on the tradition as a result of his recordings and preaching tours.

the black folktales about the biblical characters; but in interpreting the stories, he sets them in the historical context of the biblical age and explains the characters' behavior in terms of historical as well as psychological context. At the same time, he is a master storyteller, and each of his sermons turns on the Bible story that dramatized the Scripture passage he chose. The close of the sermon, when he becomes the poet and begins to chant and sing, usually revolves around another story, related to the Bible story but outside of the Bible, a personal experience or a parable from the secular world—for example, the story of the mother's sacrifice for her son that closed his Mother's Day sermon.

I first learned of Reverend Franklin in the late 1960s. I was playing guitar with a Minneapolis blues band and the leader, Lazy Bill Lucas, also played piano in a local Baptist church; we went there together one Sunday and I heard the improvised, chanted prayers and sermon. In his sermon, the preacher, Rev. George Trawick, alternated periods of speech with periods of a raspy, tuneful chant, and the congregation responded at the ends of his phrases with cries (right on the tonic pitch) of "Preach!," "Yes, Lord!," "Yeah!," and "Come on!" I had never seen or heard anything like it, and I asked Bill about it. He told me Aretha Franklin's father was the best preacher he had ever heard, and that he had some record albums out. I bought a few and was thrilled to find Franklin combining the persuasive powers of the orator with the ecstasy of the poet; more, he seemed to be singing his sermons. A graduate student in English and American Studies then, I thought of ancient bards and ritual drama, the beginnings of literature. Surely there was some connection to Reverend Franklin and the tradition he represented.

Storytelling is the key technique in the black sermon. As E. Franklin Frazier pointed out, slavemasters, mistresses, and ministers told slaves stories about heroes and villains, reward and punishment in the Bible.[6] The stories went around, slave exhorters reinforced them, and for the slaves the biblical people became familiar folk heroes, the stuff of folktales. They admired Moses who led the Jews out of slavery and David who defeated Goliath against all odds. From then on, black preachers have dramatized the Bible by preaching about these characters—Jacob and Esau, Adam and Eve, Solomon, Moses, David, and, of course, Jesus—examining their motives and behavior as if they were contemporaries, which in a sense they are.

In his sermons, Franklin gives voice to

By the mid-1970s when I interviewed him, Franklin was in his early sixties, and if his delivery was slower than it had been, his oratory was more persuasive.[7] The congregation numbered about three thousand,

and his church was a regular Sunday stopping off place for visitors to Detroit. They wanted to see and hear the man once known as "the jitterbug preacher" because he was so stylish and handsome; the man whose sermons, recorded live, were available on several dozen record albums; the man whose unprecedented preaching tours, from the mid-1950s through the mid-1960s, brought him to halls, civic auditoriums, and stadiums in every black community in the United States; and the man whose leadership of the historic 1963 freedom march in Detroit attracted two hundred thousand people and provided the prototype for the march later that summer in Washington led by the Reverend Martin Luther King, Jr.

Franklin was born in 1915 in Sunflower County, near Indianola, Mississippi, not far from where the great blues singer B. B. King was born. It is an apt comparison, for just as tens of thousands of blues guitarists imitated King, so tens of thousands of preachers imitated Franklin. Rev. Stanley Picard, pastor of the 25th Street Church of God in Christ, in Detroit, said, "What I like about Reverend Franklin is that he is America's greatest preacher, whether he be black, white, or indifferent. And every preacher who's ever tried to preach, somewhere has tried to preach like Reverend Franklin. My father used to say, when I was a kid and didn't know what preaching was, he said, 'The Lord knows Reverend Franklin can preach.' And my daddy knew what true preaching was."

The child, Wordsworth said, is father to the man; what was it about Rev. Clarence LaVaughn Franklin's childhood that set his course? His mother, Rachel Franklin, remembered him as a good and obedient boy but said he was "kind of a peculiar child." He wouldn't play with the other children; he sat on the Franklins' front porch while the others played marbles. Clarence loved to watch the others play, but he deliberately separated himself, according to his mother. A childhood incident underscored for him the importance of public speaking. When he was about eleven, Clarence was supposed to recite a speech at a school assembly, and his mother went over it with him carefully beforehand. But when he spoke, he mumbled and could not be heard. "So when we got home," his mother said, "we all went in the house and undressed and everything, and he was kind of slow, because he knew what was going to happen, you know? And he came on out, and I says, 'What was wrong with you tonight? You never have spoke like that.' I said, 'Do you know nobody understood what you were out there saying?' And I said, 'You didn't even open your mouth. What is wrong?' And he just dropped his head. I think he was very sorry he did that, you know? But I had to talk to him about it, and then get hold of him about it. And I told him. I shook my finger. I said, 'From now on I bet you'll open your mouth.' And he has been opening it ever since!"

Clarence's stepfather, Henry Franklin, was a sharecropper, and the family worked hard to make ends meet; even during good years they did not clear a profit. I asked Reverend Franklin about his childhood memories.

I remember one thing that stands out from after my mother remarried. My father used to go to the commissary. The boss owned the commissary, and he would get his groceries there. The boss would charge him against the crop. Now my father, like many of the sharecroppers, was completely illiterate, to the point that he couldn't even write his name. And of course not being able to read or figure except a bit in his own head, he never really knew what we owed. At the end of the year, which they called on the farm *settling time*, families would total up, and the boss would total up the bales of cotton that had been gathered. Now in our case if we made twenty to twenty-five bales of cotton during the year, the boss would say, "Well, Henry, you didn't come out. But we'll just call it even and start fresh next year."

Now this went on year after year.

I remember Christmas morning. My mother would cry because the only thing that she could purchase for the children were raisins and oranges and apples and striped candy. No toys. I never had toys. But I was very anxious about Christmas morning, even to get the oranges and the apples, the raisins and the candy. I never will forget that striped candy.

And that stands out: her crying.

Rachel took young Clarence to church, and at age nine he decided to become a member. Speaking to me in Detroit more than fifty years later, he said he never fell under conviction, never felt condemned by God, never felt that he was in danger of going to hell. "It seemed to me that God had provided all of the things *for* me, including his love, and now it was time to respond." Unlike many of the others at St. Peter's Rock Baptist Church, in Cleveland, Mississippi, his conversion was not outwardly emotional; he simply stepped forward from the mourners' bench at a revival. "My conversion was not unusual or spectacular. When the minister finished his sermon and invited us to come, I simply got up and went to the altar. There were a lot of people who adhered to the tradition of black people; some were rather expressive, shouting and what have you, crying and going on. And some were not." Like the child on the porch watching the other children play marbles, Franklin must have been at once emotionally engaged and simultaneously controlled and detached during his conversion—qualities that would serve him well in preaching, where at moments of great emotional intensity, locked with the congregation in a driving, rhythmic embrace as he proceeds from one line to the next, he cannot falter and must retain command of what he is saying so that it makes sense.

As a teenager, Clarence first gained a local reputation as a singer, joining the choir at St. Peter's Rock and in a few years becoming a soloist. Hearing him sing, it is easy to tell where Aretha got her voice. His singing can be heard on several of his sermon albums, for he always prefaced a sermon with a traditional "meter hymn" such as "Father, I stretch my hand to thee" or "I heard the voice of Jesus say," and sometimes moved into a gospel hymn such as "Precious Lord" after the close of the sermon during the Invitation. At least two albums feature him and his daughter singing. His is a full baritone voice, with great strength and volume, and the kind of buzzing raspiness at moments of intensity that signals feeling in black singing, whether it be Bessie Smith singing blues or Rev. Julius

Cheeks singing gospel—the same buzzing raspiness that is a benchmark in certain kinds of African music.

In his mid-teens Clarence felt himself called by God to the ministry. He was inspired by watching the other preachers at St. Peter's Rock, and one minister in particular impressed him: Rev. Benjamin J. Perkins, the president of the state Baptist convention. One night in his sleep he had a dream or vision in which he saw a plank on fire but not being consumed, and from behind the plank a voice spoke to him and said, "Go and preach the gospel to all nations." He spoke to his mother about the experience the next day and, with her encouragement, talked to his pastor and later preached a successful trial sermon. At that point there were numerous teenage black preachers in the Mississippi Delta—many more than the churches could support—so he became a lay preacher at St. Peter's Rock.

Clarence had been to school during the winter months when he wasn't needed on the farm, but his father had in mind that he would be a farmer, not a preacher. His father was not a member of a church and felt that farming must come first. Clarence, out plowing, left mule and plow in the middle of the field and climbed on a stump whenever the Spirit moved him to preach. The conflict between father and son continued. Knowing what he did about the plantation system, the powerlessness of the sharecroppers, and the segregated society, Clarence did not want to be a farmer. "I couldn't see any future in farming. My father was never a successful farmer in terms of economics. There were other people that I could contrast with him, a few successful farmers who owned land, who had cars and trucks, but my father never reached that point. And I had grown up on a farm and I didn't particularly like farming."

Wanderlust overcame him, and he longed to travel. He ran away to an aunt in Shelby, Mississippi, and then joined two of his uncles and their families to go off to

*Franklin with his wife, Barbara, in Detroit in the late 1940s. Courtesy of Rachel Franklin*

*Franklin with his children: Cecil, Erma, Carolyn, and Aretha. Detroit in the early 1950s. Courtesy of Erma Franklin*

Missouri as migrant farm hands. They stayed a season in Missouri, then went to Kentucky, and wound up in Michigan picking strawberries. Clarence was not a dependable worker because he sometimes took to preaching in the middle of a field, but whenever they needed a preacher for a Sunday sermon he was willing and able. He went south to Arkansas and stayed with relatives awhile, then returned home to Cleveland, Mississippi, where he was ordained as a minister at St. Peter's Rock.

Living at home must have been difficult

for him. Torn between his calling to preach and his father's need for him on the farm, he tried to do both, preaching at various churches and even holding down a pastorate for about six months in nearby Tutwiler, Mississippi. Trying to impress them as a pastor, he preached long and hard one Sunday, "and the next morning I got the bus going back to Cleveland," he said.

But my bus was late, and when I got home, my father—I got home around nine o'clock that morning. Well, he'd been in the field since seven or seven-thirty, and he said, "Now this going off preaching and coming in this time of day is no good." Said, "Now you have got to make up your mind whether you want to preach or plow."

So I made up my mind that very day, and left home with virtually nothing. And I went down and talked with a blind friend of mine who was very active in our church, an astute man named Jim. And Jim said, "Well, son, you can stay here with me until you find a place."

For the next few years Reverend Franklin preached in Cleveland and Clarksdale, eventually coming to pastor a church near Shelby. He met and married his wife Barbara, and their first child, Erma, was born. Realizing he needed more education, Franklin, aged about twenty-one, took his family to Greenville and enrolled in Greenville Industrial College, a new institution underwritten by the state's Baptist Convention that offered courses in theology and trades. He learned that a sermon should be prepared ahead of time, that it should have an introduction, a body, and a climax, and that it was best delivered from memory, although not memorized; in other words, prepared and remembered rather than read from notes. The Greenville theologians were fundamentalists and Franklin adopted that point of view.

Dorothy Swan, director of the Bulletin Club at New Bethel, the church's publicity organization, knew Franklin during this period and recalled that he was already a phenomenon, preaching in Greenville and Clarksdale and occasionally in Memphis. Never preaching from notes, Franklin "had a memory" and was already chanting his sermons. Whooping, zooning (or zooming), and tuning were names that preachers and congregations gave to the technique of chanting, and some thought that chanting signaled that the message was coming directly from the Holy Spirit, with the preacher serving as a medium. Franklin was thrilled with his power to move people, particularly to get the elders to shout; Dorothy Swan said he "wanted to tickle the grandmas on the street," to reach the masses, and after he preached at a revival in Memphis, one hundred people who came to the altar were saved.

It wasn't long before Franklin was invited to pastor in Memphis, but when he and his family moved there—he was about twenty-four—he encountered skepticism from other ministers who were more modern, learned, and sophisticated than this country preacher. Franklin's response was to seek more education, and he enrolled as a special student in LeMoyne College for three years, studying English literature and sociology, taking two or three classes per day while attending to his ministerial duties on evenings and weekends. He also attended the Howe School of Religion. "I would characterize myself as a fundamentalist prior to coming to Memphis," Franklin said.

But then I began to be exposed to new interpretations, and I started to go to LeMoyne, and I was exposed to new biblical views, and I started traveling, and came into contact with preachers around the country when I would go and run revivals and speak at ministers' conferences. And they would visit with me, usually several preachers daily. And we had discussions, both in the conferences and at the private home where I was stopping, or the hotel.

And my views and interpretations and understanding began to evolve. Of course this aroused within me some concern about my former views, but I regarded it more or less as a deepening. At that time my sermons may have begun to become more historically minded and less evangelical. Evangelism to me is simply stirring people up, to make them feel some spontaneous thing that may not be lasting, while if you preach to them in terms of the historical meaning it's altogether different. It has a more lasting effect because you're reaching their minds as well as their emotions.

In Mississippi I might have been more interested in reaching their emotions. I was what they called a Spiritual preacher. That meant that if you preached in such a way with an intonation—what you [J. T. T.] call chant—and what you were saying had meaning for them and moved them, then you were a Spiritual preacher.

"Did it have anything to do with the Spirit of the Lord?" I asked.

"Well, they felt so. It worked in their response. That's the way it manifested itself in them, because what they felt, they expressed."

"But what about you?" I pursued. "Some people believe that the whooping part of the sermon is the voice of the Spirit."

Franklin laughed. "Yes, yes," he said.

"You were skeptical even then?"

"No, I wasn't skeptical then," he admitted. "I accepted it as a matter of course at that time. But then one grows. And as I went along, I discovered that the emotional thing was short-lived. I saw people who would express those kinds of emotions yet were not changed at all. It's all right to do it; it's all right for one to express himself in that manner, shouting and all that. But I would like for him to have something mentally that would be lasting, because the mental can be spiritual, even more spiritual than the emotional.

"My feeling about the Spirit and the preacher *now*," Franklin went on, "is that the Spirit inspires you beyond what you have read, enlightens you, and gives you strength. But I do not feel when I preach that the Spirit is *controlling* what I am saying."

As Franklin's knowledge grew his sermons became more sophisticated theologically and historically, and they began to take on the literary and psychological power that characterized them in later

*Franklin outside his home in Detroit, the late 1950s. Courtesy of Erma Franklin*

years. In other words, listening to them persuaded both the head and heart. Their theme never wavered; however learned Franklin became, his message was conservative: no matter how difficult life seems, have faith and trust in God the father.

In the early 1940s Franklin sang and preached on a weekly radio show in Memphis. I do not know the details of the program, but it may have been one of the earliest instances of a regular black radio ministry. During the Memphis years the other Franklin children were born—Cecil, Aretha, and Carolyn. Barbara Franklin, who sang and played piano in the church, enrolled at LeMoyne also and was extremely busy taking care of four children and a husband at the same time. Dorothy Swan remembers good times when she would bring a washboard and pail to the Franklins and she and Barbara did their combined wash together, talking and laughing so hard that the clothes splashed out of the pails.

At twenty-seven Franklin accepted an offer to be the minister of the Friendship Baptist Church in Buffalo, New York. Moving there with his family, he continued his studies at the University of Buffalo, majoring in literature. Friendship was a large church, better off financially than Franklin's Memphis churches; most of the parishioners had migrated from the South, and they had

*Franklin listens to the play-back of one of his sermons on tape at the J-V-B recording company in Detroit in the early 1950s. Joe Von Battle operates the machine. Photograph by Edward McLaughlin, courtesy of Erma Franklin*

found better wages and job security at Bethlehem Steel and the automobile plants and other factories in the area. But the climate was too cold and damp for Franklin, and he began to develop the bronchitis that plagued him from then on. Besides, he felt isolated from the mainstream of black life. "I didn't like preaching in Buffalo because of the conservative, staid, frontier type of life there," he said. "I wanted to be in a more fluid situation. By that I mean I wanted to be in a city where there were crossroads of transportation. Trains, buses, planes, where people are coming and going, conventions of all kinds, and migrations. I wanted a city not static in its growth. People weren't coming in and out of Buffalo as they would Detroit or Chicago or New York. . . . I felt kind of cut off from the on-flow of life in this country."

Franklin preached at the National Baptist Convention in Detroit in 1945, and the following year he agreed to become pastor of New Bethel Baptist Church, arriving in June. He liked the congregation but was

dissatisfied with the church building, a storefront on Hastings Street. During the next few years they raised funds for a new building and arrangements were made to have it constructed on the old site, but after the old building was torn down the construction company did not finish the new one and the congregation had to meet at different church buildings in the area for the next several years. To raise more money Franklin began a radio broadcast in 1951 and the congregation increased tremendously. Soon they obtained a high-interest loan and completed the church on Hastings Street.

I asked Franklin how his sermon recordings came about:

One night I was preaching on the air, and a guy down the street, a black man named Joe Battles [Joe Von Battle], he was coming

*Funeral home owner Benjamin McFall, Rev. Martin Luther King, Jr., and Rev. C. L. Franklin. In early June 1963, King was in Detroit for a civil rights march organized by Franklin, "A Walk for Freedom," which attracted 200,000 participants. King gave his "I Have a Dream" speech at this event, thus before its Washington, D.C., presentation. Photograph by Edwards Photo. Courtesy of Erma Franklin*

from Inkster and was listening. And he came on to the church, and after the dismissal he came up to me and said, "Man, the way these people come out here to hear you and listen to you, if you would record this, people would buy it." Said, "Why don't you let me tape your sermons? I have a little rapport with Chess Recording Company. I know the man, I knew him when he got started, and I helped him a great deal. I'm sure that he would consider it."

I didn't think too much of it right then. I said, "We'll get together and sit down and go over the idea and see what we can come up with."

So a few days later we talked. He went about it, taped the sermons, went to Chicago, contacted Chess, and came back with a contract. I signed, he managed, and, of course, the thing mushroomed.

Indeed it did mushroom. Radio station WLAC-AM in Nashville, a clear-channel,

50,000-watt station that could be heard throughout the nation at night, began playing his sermon records, and the program sponsor, Randy's Record Shop, advertised them for sale. Franklin received invitations to preach in towns and cities all over the United States. He began by joining the Clara Ward Singers but soon directed his own preaching tours, and from about 1954 until about 1965, when he cut back on the tours for health reasons, Chess kept releasing his new sermon records and he preached throughout the nation, returning one or two Sundays per month to preach at New Bethel. The New Bethel congregation grew to ten thousand, and added to that were thousands of visitors to Detroit who came to hear him preach. The building was far too small, and the church had to set up loudspeakers in the streets outside. What

an event this must have been, month after month, year after year. Meanwhile, Aretha was singing gospel music on the preaching tours and gaining a reputation as a fine singer in her own right.

As the Civil Rights Movement grew, Franklin embraced the nonviolent resistance philosophy of Rev. Martin Luther King, Jr. In 1963 he invited King to accompany him in a civil rights march in Detroit. King accepted. They drew two hundred thousand people and King read the same speech he read later that summer in Washington: *I Have a Dream.* "Dr. King sat right in my basement one Sunday night," Franklin said. "He had spoken for my Men's Day, and he said, 'Frank, I will never live to see forty. Some of our white brothers are very, very sick, and they are dangerous. I'll never see forty.' And he was thirty-nine when he was killed."

Franklin was a member of SCLC, and later joined PUSH, Rev. Jesse Jackson's organization, but political activism *per se* took a back seat to his chief missions, preaching and pastoral care, as he led New Bethel through the turbulent sixties. He told me what happened one night when one of the more radical Black Power groups confronted the police at New Bethel.

*Franklin preaching, Little Rock Baptist Church, Detroit, October 2, 1977. Photograph by Jeff Titon*

In Detroit there was a movement called the New Republic of Africa. I had no affiliation with that particular group. But they rented the church, and it was on a Saturday night, 1968 sometime. The only member of our church that was there was the janitor. And of course about twelve o'clock [Deacon] Ben Washington called me and told me, "Reverend, Reverend, you'd better get up and come down here. There's been some shooting down here!"

And I said, "Shooting?"

Said, "You know that movement that rented the church? They had some kind of shooting with the police!"

Well, the police apparently had had them under surveillance for quite some time before, and they were circulating in the community, around the church. And they had guards, armed guards, for the officials of this movement. These guys had on fatigue boots, and uniforms, and something like berets, and they had these rifles on their shoulders.

So when I got down there, I went into the church, went into the lobby, and attempted to go into the sanctuary. The head policeman, the one that was apparently in charge, said, "You can't go in."

I said, "Why? There's no shooting. Nobody's in there."

"Well, they're cleaning up now."

The police, what they were really doing, they were gathering the bullets that had lodged in the benches. Nobody was hurt, fortunately, in there. What precipitated the whole thing was that these movement officials were getting into their cars, with their guards standing by, and when the police got

out of their cars with their guns, these guys just started shooting, outside.

The people were still in the church. Just the officials coming out. And they shot a policeman. The other policeman that was in the car with the one that got shot called for help, and they were right there within a minute and a half, right at the church. And they came in shooting.

Someone called out, "Get on the floor! Get on the floor!" And they were shooting all through there. The pulpit desk had several holes in it.

They said there was a shootout, but really there was no shootout. Most of the glass was inside the lobby and, as I showed the police commissioner, in the back pews, the pews near the entrance into the auditorium, the splinters were lying in the seats. There were no splinters back of the benches, which meant that the shooting was coming inside rather than coming outside. The policemen were doing the shooting. There wasn't any physical sign of any shots going out of the church. But, you know, the police are going to respond when that policeman got shot. And that was outside.

I went upstairs to the office, and [minister of music] Shelby was sitting there fanning: "Ooh my God, ooh Lawd, who let those people have the church? Ooh my God, they torn up our church!"

I said, "Shelby, we are in the throes of a revolution, a social revolution. Some people have lost their lives in this revolution, and we have lost a little glass. I think we got out cheap."

In the 1970s Franklin stopped his preaching tours and concentrated on his New Bethel ministry. The congregation fell to about three thousand—still a large church, one of the largest in Detroit—and Franklin received the recognition due him as an elder statesman in the black community. In 1977 I watched him preach as the guest of honor at a Senior Citizens Day in Inkster, a suburb north of Detroit. Franklin drove me out there, and on the way I asked him how he would sum up his views about God. "Predestination is not a part of my preaching," he said.

I cannot believe that God has, for example, predestined that a train would run over you, and then see him as a loving God. What father would plan for the destruction of his son? That would be a contradiction in the character of God to me.

Some people even now think they should do good because they are afraid God will take vengeance upon them if they do differently. But I don't think that one should embrace God in terms of fear. I think one should embrace God in terms of love. I believe that God is love, and that God is a father, and we are pictured as his children. I cannot think of God being a father and the epitome of love, and just because his children happen to be contrary and unruly sometimes, that he will put them into eternal punishment. I can't see that. I'm a better father than that!

"On the basis of what the Lord has promised even to me,

give me this mountain."

He looked toward a mountain range of about five or more cities and said,

"Now I would like to settle on those mountains. I'd like

to spend my last days on the mountains. I would like

for my family to be left with the inheritance of a mountain.

Therefore give me the mountain." Dr. Caldwell. "Give me the mountain."

I thought of Franklin's own father, who left Mississippi just after Clarence was born, and joined the American troops in Europe during World War I. Coming back after the war, he felt that sharecropping in Mississippi was too confining, particularly, as Franklin said, "after having seen the big cities, and having ridden on the ocean liners, and having been to Paris." He left and Rachel remarried, and Franklin had had his problems with his stepfather, running away from home, returning and eventually over his father's objections choosing to preach, not to plow. In the picture of God as a loving father he found an image of a wise elder, a strong and benevolent and loving presence who would be a constant companion.

Early in the morning of June 10, 1979, three men and two women parked a white 1967 Chevrolet outside of Reverend Franklin's Detroit home. Franklin was in his upstairs bedroom, for it was his habit to stay up late at night, sometimes reading theology, sometimes watching the late show. The three men broke in and made some noise while trying to steal antique leaded glass windows. Hearing them, Franklin took a pistol and went out to the landing. Two of the burglars shot him, one in the knee and the other in the groin. As he fell on the landing the burglars escaped. Several hours later a neighbor found Franklin where he fell. Taken to the emergency ward, he had lost a lot of blood; he was unconscious and in critical condition. Without being on life-sustaining apparatus he remained in a coma for five years until he died on July 27, 1984. His funeral was the largest that Detroit has ever seen.

It is not easy to sum up his legacy as a preacher, but his place in the history of the black American church is secure, while his sermons cry out for a wider audience. He was, after all, one of the masterful preacher-poets of this century, and it is only a matter of time before this recognition comes his way. As I have suggested, the black American sermon is a combination of reason (spoken oratory) and faith (chanted poetry). For the believer, the reasoned language of the church—oratory and the language of the Bible—permeates daily life, shapes daily thought and utterance. The language of faith—the cry to God in prayer, the sermon's chanted poem—is, on the other hand, an extraordinary, ecstatic response to the mysteries of faith, and it thrusts the believer back into the source of belief, feeling the power of God. Making and remaking black folktales as the stuff of his sermons, Franklin told and chanted stories to both ends, oratory and poetry, and his sermons stand as exemplars, both as expressions of the black American experience and as a human response to his own struggles and to the struggles of his people.

NOTES

1. This article is part of my forthcoming two-volume book on the Reverend C. L. Franklin. Quoted material is from interviews and sermons I recorded in Detroit in 1976, 1977, and 1978. I am grateful for a pilot grant from the Folk/Jazz/Ethnic division of the National Endowment for the Arts and a fellowship for independent study and research from the National Endowment for the Humanities which made the field research possible. I am grateful also to Samuel Jenkins and Rachel Franklin for their help during the period of field research, and to Erma Franklin for her cooperation and the photographs she supplied. I am most grateful to Reverend Franklin himself, who took many hours from his busy schedule to talk with me about his life and preaching.

2. *A Journey in the Back Country* (New York: Mason Bros., 1860), 187.

3. *The Art of the American Folk Preacher* (New York: Oxford Univ. Press, 1970), 13–16.

4. *I Got the Word in Me and I Can Sing It, You Know* (Philadelphia: Univ. of Pennsylvania Press, 1985), 10.

5. See Edwin A. Smith, *Aggrey of Africa: A Study in Black and White* (London: Student Christian Movement Press, 1929).

6. *The Negro Church in America* (New York: Schocken Books, 1964), 9.

7. An account of my first meeting with Reverend Franklin was published in "Stance, Role, and Identity in Fieldwork among Folk Baptists and Pentecostals in the United States," *American Music* 3 (1985):16–24.

# A Mother at the Cross

*Sermon by the Reverend C. L. Franklin,*
*New Bethel Baptist Church, Detroit, Michigan, May 14, 1978.*
*Field videotape recording and transcription by Jeff Todd Titon.*

I want to talk with you this evening from a passage found in the book of St. John, the nineteenth chapter, the twenty-fifth and the twenty, through the twenty-seventh verse. "Now there stood by the cross of Jesus his mother, and his mother's sister, Mary the wife of Cleophas, and Mary Magdalene. When Jesus therefore saw his mother, and the disciple standing by, whom he loved, he said unto his mother, Woman, behold thy son! Then said he to the disciple, Behold thy mother! And from that hour the disciple took her unto his own home."

Now I want to talk about a mother at the Cross. I think the thing that makes us identify ourselves with Jesus is because of his humanness. I thank God that he didn't make him without the tendency of temptation. I thank God that the Lord made him in such a way that he got hungry, he got tired, he got sleepy, he got lonely. He wept, cried like you cry sometimes.

In this instance he did something very characteristic of himself, that under the spell of excruciating pain, in an hour when he felt like even God had forsaken him, when darkness was not only upon him physically but darkness was upon him mentally and spiritually. We have those hours sometime with us, for in our lives some rain falls, some winds blow, some storms arise. But characteristic, characteristic of him because under those unusual circumstances he thought about others: he thought about his mother.

Now his mother had been with him from birth. She was at the cradle, she was in the home, she was in and out of the carpenter's shop. She walked backwards and forward to Jerusalem along with him. Those were not hard places, bad places, but the thing that makes this experience unique is that she was not only at all of these other places, she was at the cross. (I don't believe you're praying with me tonight.)[1]

She was at the cross. Now there are some theological commentators who said that while Peter had denied him and many of the others had deserted him and Judas had betrayed him, Mary was there—. Some of the commentators say that she was there because she was permitted to be there under the cultural situation, that women were not thought of as equals in anything: in responsibility or anything else. It is said that women were almost unnoticed. But this is a sad commentary.

Anytime a man has been charged with treason—hmm? Anytime the Roman government has ruled that you are guilty of treason, it's dangerous for anybody to be with you. (Did you hear me?) Anytime the Jewish church had decreed that he was a heretic, an impostor, and a devil—I want to tell you, it was dangerous for Mary to be there.

You know, if you've read this Scripture with any care, the Scripture surrounding the trial and crucifixion of Jesus, the arrest, the trial, and the crucifixion, you'll notice that the charge was first a religious charge. He had blasphemed against God, according to the high priests. But the country, Judea, although the Jews had some rights, they did not have the right of capital punishment. (Did you hear me?)

And of course when they came up with that charge, Herod wouldn't deal with it. "Now you've got to get us another charge. Now whatever he's done to offend you-all here in your church, we can't deal with that. It's certainly not deserving capital punishment. If you want him put to death you got to come up with a better charge than that." And they went back and brought up treason, saying that he was working against Caesar. He was working against the state. He was inspiring and instigating a revolution against Rome. Then Caesar said, "Well now—" or Pilate said, "Well, I can deal with that now. If he's, if he's doing anything against the state, then we can deal with him."

Now I'm trying to say that through it all, Mary was there. His mother was there. Jesus, I mean Cecil[2] talked about the qualifications of a mother this morning, and motherhood was not just something biological, but is something that one has to earn. Just because you have had a child doesn't make you a mother! Motherhood is something that one has to achieve. Well, I'm trying to tell you that Mary was a model mother. She not only brought him into this world, she taught him the traditions of his people. She saw to it that he observed all of the rites, all of the ceremonies. And here at the end, she was there. Didn't have the privilege of being at his bedside. It was worse than that. She was standing by his cross.

Say, "Well, why wasn't she scared?" Love rules out fear. Say, "Well, he has broken the law." Love doesn't care anything about breaking the law. Some folks say, "I love you when you're right, but when you're wrong I'm through with you." Then you don't love. (You don't hear me.) Because if you love me, you're with me right or wrong. You're there to help me get strength if I'm wrong.

She was at his cross. Her sister was there, and then Mary Magdalene was there. Her sister, who was the mother of James and John, had come to him one day and said, "Well now, I know that you are going to follow the Messianic tradition and I know you're about to get your kingdom set up and organized. I want my two sons to be closest to the throne. I want James on one side. I want John on the other. Don't have too much time to worry about other folks' children; I'm talking about mine." Jesus pointed out to her the selfishness of her ambition but it didn't crush her, for she was working for her own children; she was functioning as a mother. (You don't hear me tonight. Listen if you please.)

I believe it was Rudyard Kipling who said,

If I were hanged from the highest hill,
   Mother, o mother of mine;
I know whose love would follow me still,
   Mother, o mother of mine.
If I were damned—or drowned, rather, in
   the deepest sea,
   Mother, o mother of mine;
I know whose love would come down to
   me,
   Mother, o mother of mine.
If I were damned of body and soul,
   Mother, o mother of mine;
I know whose prayers would make me
whole,
Mother of mine, o mother of mine.

She was at the cross. I tell you, if one is in the deepest sea, she's there or her prayers are there. If you're damned body and soul, her love and prayers will make you whole. (You don't hear me.)

So Jesus said, "Woman," which was not derogatory, considering it within the framework of his culture. It was not disrespectful. He said, "Woman, behold your son." Said, "Now I know I'm about to leave here. I'm hanging from a tree. And my weight is tearing the flesh in my hands. But I want to see that you have a home before I leave here. I want you to have somewhere to go. Now I've got some brothers but I can't leave you with my brothers because they don't believe in me." (I wished I had somebody here to pray.) "I want to leave you with somebody who believes that God has wrought a miracle in my life." (You don't hear me today.)

That was one of the things he said from the cross. Another one, I said he was concerned about others, another one was, "Father forgive them, for they know not what they do." And then, "Verily I say unto thee, today thou shalt be with me in Paradise." And then, "Father, into thine hands I commend my spirit." These were things that he said while he was dying.

Somebody said he stopped dying long enough to run revival and take one of the thieves along with him. (You don't hear me.) Stopped dying and prayed for them, and said, "This day you'll be with me in Paradise." And then he said, right after he appointed Mary a home, "I thirst. I've been out here since noon, hanging on this tree. I've been out here under unusual tropical sun. I've been losing blood since last night. But I wanted to get at least one of the thieves straight. And then I wanted to pray for everybody who's doing things against themselves and others. I wanted to pray for them before it's over. And then I want to commit and commend my spirit to God." And certainly he did. And when he said that, he dropped his head, and said, "It's finished. The battle is over. The task has been completed. The work has been done. To this end was I born.

"And
    for this cause
        came I
        into the world.
And
    it's finished now.
O Lord.
    I don't need
        anybody
        to commit me.
    I don't need
        anybody
        to read the burial ceremony.
Well
    I'm going to say it
        myself.
Yes I am.
    Into your hands
        I commend my spirit.
O Lord."
And
    I remember reading
        a story a long time ago
        that dealt with
    mother's eternal love.
    It is said
        that her son
        was in jail,
    and he was in there
        because he had been condemned
        to die.

O Lord.
    They were going to put a rope
        around his neck
and
    the hangsman
    was going to remove
    the plank on which he was standing.
O Lord.
    And
    they
    had tried
        and failed
        time and again
        to get him a reprieve.
O Lord.
    And every time
        they failed.
O Lord.
    The mother
    thought about an old
        tradition
        that went on and obtained
        in that country:
    before they hanged
anybody
    they had to ring the bell.
O Lord.
    And early that morning
        she got up
    and went down
        to the courthouse
        where
        the gallows had been situated.

**NOTES**

1. I have put these direct addresses to the congregation in parentheses. Franklin told me he sometimes uses them to gain time, and sometimes to ask for more amens from the congregation when he feels they are not paying close attention. The congregation members know what he wants and respond more fully—for awhile, at any rate.

2. Cecil Franklin, Reverend Franklin's son, spoke in church that morning.

A note on the transcription format: for the sake of readability, I have rendered the spoken part of the sermon as prose and the chanted part as poetry. (The Kipling poem is spoken, however.)

I divide Franklin's chant into lines based on his pauses for breath; that is, I stop each line where he stops for breath and I begin again on the line below, where he begins again after taking a breath. By its music, Franklin's chant falls into three types of lines or, as I will indicate here, musical phrases: auxiliary, main, and secondary phrases.

One type of phrase is brief and formulaic (e.g., "O Lord"), tends to gain Franklin time, and establishes the tonic pitch by ending strongly on the tonic. This type I call "auxiliary" and set it flush against the left margin. Another type of phrase starts at or quickly rises to the pitch apex (i.e., the highest pitch) and then falls toward the tonic, usually by thirds (e.g., 5–3–3–1). This type I call "main" and set it indented from the left margin. I set "secondary phrases" as lines indented further from the left margin. This third type of phrase follows a main phrase and has a pitch apex below the preceding main phrase's pitch apex, usually a minor third above the tonic. Secondary phrases usually end on the tonic.

(The main phrase's pitch apex increases as the chanted section progresses. At the beginning, Franklin establishes a main phrase pitch apex a minor or neutral third above the tonic; very soon after, he moves the pitch apex up to a perfect fifth above the tonic; toward the end of the

O Lord.
    She climbed up
    in the belfry
        about an hour
        before time.
O Lord.
    And
    then the hangman
    and his crowd
        came marching out.
And
    she was up in the belfry
    holding on
        to the bell clapper.
O Lord.
    They got the rope
        in their hands.
    They pulled down
        but there was no sound.
    And as they pulled the bell,
    the bell swung over
        from one side to another.
O Lord.
    She fell
    against the iron wall
        of that big bell.
    O Lord.
    She was bruised,
    she was bleeding,
    but she held on
        to the bell clapper,
    oh yes she did.
    Yes.

And after awhile
    they gave up.
After awhile
they said, "Since the bell won't ring,
    we can't execute him."
O Lord.
    By that time
    she fell down
        upon the ground
        under the bell clapper
    with blood
    running from her nose,
    from her eyes
        and from her shoulders.
O Lord.
    She said, "Well, son,
    I know you meant good.
    You are my child.
    Go on.
    Don't worry.
    Don't worry
    about me.
    I'm all right."
    O Lord.
    Did you know
    that Jesus,
        Jesus
    held the bell clapper
    of time and eternity
        in his hands?
    Oh well,
    ohh,
    yes!

chant he moves it up further, a minor seventh above the tonic; and sometimes at the very end the apex is an octave above the tonic. His daughter, Erma, likened the process to shifting gears in an automobile.)

Often there is a grammatical correspondence: auxiliary phrases are formulas or conjunctions; main phrases carry subject and verb; secondary phrases carry objects and prepositional phrases. This correspondence tends to collapse near the sermon's close when most of the lines have the pitch apex and thus fall into main phrases.

Here is an example:

| O Lord. | [auxiliary] |
| And | [auxiliary] |
|     I remember reading | [main] |
|         a story a long time ago | [secondary] |
|         that dealt with | [secondary] |
|     mother's eternal love. | [main] |

It is possible to set this several different ways, and over the past fifteen years or so I have experimented with and published ethnopoetic transcriptions in which whole sermons are set as poetry, and I have used devices such as italics, boldface, and capital letters to indicate volume. I have slanted the lines on the page to follow intonation, and at times I have used musical notation along with the text of the chant. All of these settings have their uses, providing, as it were, a kind of performance score.

The setting here is less radical because, although I agree with Dennis Tedlock (who has written much on this question) that prose on the page is a poor medium to present the spoken word, I chose readability over oratorical performance. The poetry I happily set as poetry, influenced by William Carlos Williams's idea of the "variable foot" and Charles Olson's idea of "projective verse." And in an age when inexpensive videotape can bring voice and gesture into one's living room (I hope to publish the videotape of *A Mother at the Cross*, for example), an ethnopoetic score now seems almost as anachronistic as print itself.

# John Henry Faulk

## An Interview

BY JAMES MCNUTT

J ohn Henry Faulk has had a singularly flamboyant career as entertainer, political activist, and regional spokesman. Though probably known most widely for his appearances on the "Hee-Haw" television variety show and for his long battle against AWARE, Inc., a self-appointed Communist watch organization that attempted to blackball him from radio, Faulk did not enter the public arena as a professional entertainer or as a political activist but as a folklorist. He received an M.A. degree from the University of Texas and later taught there in the Department of English. A friend and contemporary of Alan Lomax, he was well acquainted with the previous generation of Texas folklorists, including John A. Lomax, Sr., J. Frank Dobie, and Mody Boatright.

John A. Lomax, Sr., published his *Cowboy Songs* in 1910 with an introduction by Theodore Roosevelt. He "discovered" the well-known folksinger "Leadbelly" and promoted his work. Lomax was honorary con-

*At John Henry Faulk's home in Austin, Texas, 1955. Standing: Faulk and Roy Bedichek; seated: Walter Prescott Webb, Mody Boatwright, and J. Frank Dobie. Courtesy of James McNutt*

sultant to the Archive of American Folk-Song at the Library of Congress (now the Archive of Folk Culture) from 1933 until 1942. J. Frank Dobie was an internationally known anecdotist, folkstory author, and scholar who began his long association with the University of Texas in 1914. He was a self-styled maverick who disdained the Ph.D. but gained a reputation for his knowledge of American culture that led to his appointment to the Chair of American History at Cambridge University and as honorary consultant in American cultural history at the Library of Congress. Mody Boatright earned his Ph.D. at the University of Texas and taught for most of his life in the Department of English at the University of Austin.

Faulk's remarks in the interview that follows richly integrate the story of his dawning awareness of folk expression, descriptions of the people who influenced him, and the complex interaction of discipline, poli-

tics, and personality. The clearest message to emerge from Faulk's varied encounters with folk and folklorists is his own faith in spoken performance as a means of effecting change. Where he once imitated folk sermons in dialect, he now—in 1987—appears on stage in the character of his former mentor, J. Frank Dobie. As folklorist, entertainer, legal wrangler, and politician, his verbal perseverance makes a sermon worth the listening.

The Archive of Folk Culture at the Library of Congress and the Barker Texas History Center at the University of Texas at Austin both house some sixty-nine field recordings of black church services, interviews, and other materials that Faulk collected in 1941. The placement of the recordings at the Library of Congress was arranged by Alan Lomax, in charge of the Archive from 1937 until 1942, who sent the recording disks for Faulk's use; Faulk requested and received duplicates of the original recordings for the University of Texas.

The interview was transcribed and edited, with Mr. Faulk's approval, from a recording made June 28, 1981, in Austin, Texas.

*Below and right: John Henry Faulk. Courtesy of James McNutt*

JM: The point . . . is that [folklore] would really be more narrow than what these people were, especially for Dobie. He claimed at times not to be a folklorist, for different reasons.

JF: Yeah.

JM: [John A.] Lomax, biographically, was a lot of other things, and the only reason I want to touch on the other things these people did is to see how it affected their folklore. So I want to know what their personal backgrounds were, their early career, you know, life, childhood, and that kind of thing. I want to know how they were educated, what they read, what influences they thought they had; I want to know how they tied into the institutions that they worked for, especially the university [of Texas], and how that affected them and whether it hindered or helped their work, and so on, and how they related to professional folklorists later.

JF: Good, good show, well you start in on me.

JM: All right. I want to talk to you not only as an [acquaintance of folklorists], but as [a folklorist]. You did a master's thesis on Negro. . . .

JF: "Ten Negro Sermons." That was [J. Frank] Dobie's and Dr. Rudolph Willard's idea. They had a meeting of the minds in few other places, but their minds met there. Willard was a medieval scholar but a very dear friend, and he got totally enchanted with the speech patterns down here, as a linguist you know, and was interested in linguistics. Then he became just utterly absorbed with the Negro religious manifestations, particularly the Negro sermons, because I had moved into that field then, and concentrated on this. And Dobie, who viewed all Yale professors as—well not all, that's an unfair thing to say—but he viewed the whole business of doctorates, [the] Ph.D., with a jaundiced eye. And so I was the one that brought them together, that's how I came to do this thesis; they both agreed that this would be one of the first of its kind ever undertaken. Dobie was all for it, so was [Walter Prescott] Webb, so was Rudolph. They formed literally one of my guiding lights in the matter.

JM: Okay, how did you first hear about folklore as a thing in itself, aside from hearing sermons and tales and songs . . .?

JF: Well you must understand that in the early thirties, there'd been a Folklore Society before that. I knew Alan Lomax—didn't know him well; he lived on the other side of town, old Mr. John A. did. And then Alan, see, went up to Choate first, and then to Harvard, but was down here a great deal because this was his home base, Austin was. And when I was a sophomore at the university, my brother had taken courses under Webb and Dobie both, and was very keen on folklore, but never active in collecting or anything. He just had an interest in it. But when I went to the university, of course, Dobie was a figure on the campus then. He had a capacity for asserting himself, and not in an abrasive way at all, but he was a literary figure. Number one, he'd had books published, he'd published in the *Saturday Evening Post;* [people would say] "that sto-

ry's published in the *Saturday Evening Post.*"

JM: [laughs]

JF: And I fell under his influence in 19—believe it was—34, yes, I'm sure it was. And Alan Lomax, I'd gotten some cedar choppers from up here in this part of the country, this was of course no Westlake Hills then, this was just mostly bootleggers and cedar choppers. Got some boys that I knew up here because they were my running mates to come down and sing—they could sing dozens, the Gant family, G.A.N.T. Ether Gant was one of the boys. And it was a singing family; they sang all the old Appalachian ballads and whatnot. I got 'em to perform, and Alan was utterly enchanted, and so he and I became very close friends, and he and his father were collecting by that time and I took Dobie's course, and Dobie and I became friends. I was a very poor student as far as the kind of scholarship that he demanded and the kind of study that he demanded, but I had the folk speech already and I was a good anecdotist and this Dobie valued very highly, so we became close personal friends. But he would ride me very hard about my slovenly habits as far as doing research and that sort of thing was concerned, and my writing, attention to the skill of writing. At that time I'd planned to be a writer and a lawyer kind of combined, and this friendship grew, and he had always a rather paternal attitude toward me and of course the great emphasis that Dobie placed on, what shall I say, on the humanity of the people that he dealt with, their songs, and their folksays, and whatnot. I didn't know Mody [Boatright] at that time. I knew of him but I didn't know him. It was Dobie and old man Lomax, and Alan that were my great friends. And old man Lomax was a very arbitrary, very kind of pompous gentleman. But a dear soul, and one of the most delicious relater of stories and observers of the folk scene that. . . . He and Alan, of course, were out with a very primitive kind of recording machine going around to the various sections of Texas and they were I'd say, the people, that took a, what shall I say, almost a scholarly interest in the collection of folklore. The Folklore Society, I joined it. And the Folklore Society consisted of half-

a-dozen or so schoolteachers and professors. It was a very esoteric study, you have
to understand, it wasn't popular, there
wasn't a widespread interest. As a matter of
fact it was considered kind of weird by
people.

JM: Well, was it like a chess club or something?

JF: Uh. . . .

JM: I mean about that level of popularity?

JF: Yes, oh yes, yes, that's quite right.
There were schoolteachers and Dobie and

Lomax. See, Lomax had broken down the,
opened the frontier, as it were, he'd made it
respectable. And a serious study. And then
there was Stith Thompson, who is from
Austin and had taught at the university and
he taught at the University of Indiana. But
his approach to the material, he was a hel-
luva nice guy, but his approach to the material was so esoteric, you know, variations
on "Froggy Went A-Courtin'" found in
Alabama and Arkansas, it just bored the
daylights out of me. It was like Rudolph
Willard studying the fragments of manu-

*Alan Lomax in a 1940
publicity photograph for
CBS. Archive of Folk Cul-
ture, Library of Congress*

scripts, illuminated manuscripts. It didn't catch me. The thing that caught me and the thing that bound Dobie and I so close together were the people themselves. Dobie was very interested in the people themselves. And interestingly enough, on a esthetic level, never on a, he never cared about how they lived, that was their business. And if they lived in hutments, he had no sociological convictions at all except that Mexicans should be Mexicans and they could sing these wonderful *corridos* and the stories they told were absolutely breathtaking. Alan Lomax was the one that had a sociological interest, and he realized that it was the expression of a people talking about themselves and the way they viewed the world and the way they viewed society and the way they viewed their own experiences in society. And, I'd say Mr. Lomax shared more of the Dobie point of view.

But I started collecting, then I went off; I went into law school, and that took my attention for about a year and I realized I wasn't going to enjoy law school and I took

a year off and traveled the country. I'd never been out of Travis County at that time. Just gone from public schools here right to the University of Texas and took it for granted that that's the way one did. In the meanwhile Alan and I stayed in correspondence, but it wasn't until 1938 when I came back, I'd decided to not go do any more law, I was going to go back into arts and science. And Dobie, as I say, Dobie and I were friends and of course Lomax and I. Daddy was a close friend of the Lomaxes and in other words, I knew them better, I knew the Lomax family much better. I thought it was very quaint that they all sang songs together. And I'll have to say, although I had a very permissive family, and a very supportive family, Mama and Daddy and all, they thought, "Oh, Johnny, you're wasting your time with those darkies, they, bless their hearts, everybody likes to hear 'em sing, but goodness don't take it seriously." And I had an ear and an eye for the unusual, the real singers. By 1938 the quartets were in great vogue, black quartets, every four blacks were a quartet. And they'd have contests, singing contests. I was going back to starting to get my bachelor's and my master's the same year, and this is when Dobie and I started seeing a lot of each other, in the late thirties.

Dobie had then become very politicized. When I first knew him he was the bane of Roy Bedichek's existence. He was not a reactionary, but he regarded Roosevelt and the New Deal and all with considerable suspicion. These were "the politicians, like buzzards come flockin' to a damn corpse, Johnny, dead horse." And Dobie had most of the cultural attitudes that a Methodist born and raised in Texas in a very Methodist family would have, and although he had moved away from religion he had the social attitudes. Segregation was perfectly acceptable to him. He never challenged it until the thirties, '36. And above all suspicions he suspected Catholics. This was very common in that day, son, you know an anti-Catholic attitude was very prevalent in the Bible Belt, the South. And Dobie retained most of those suspicions of the Catholic Church. Well, the pope of Rome blessed Franco and Hitler and Mussolini's attack on the Republic of Spain and the issues were very much like those today on the matter of El Salvador. Do we preserve this, do we help them, you know set up a fascist state, because most liberals, and I was a liberal, and certainly Mody Boatright was, whom I had met by that time, and become very fond of, he was very quiet and gentle, pipe-smoking fellow. And Roy Bedichek had very strong political opinions. When I say very strong, he didn't voice them. Now Mr. Lomax, my god he hated old Roosevelt, hated the whole damn New Deal, he was very, very conservative in his politics. His son was progressive, which he laid, Mr. Lomax laid that to the influence of Harvard University on him.

JM: Well, that's funny. I don't guess it's funny that Lomax should say that, but nothing I've seen about his experience at Harvard would indicate that. Of course he went there in 1906 and '07 . . .

JF: Oh, yeah.

JM: . . . John A. and then Alan went there in the thirties.

JF: No, no, no, you have to understand that Alan was the apple of his eye. John [A. Lomax, Jr.] was older than Alan, I think Shirley's the oldest, and then there's Johnny, who was a sweet, gentle guy whose bent went the other direction. He was kind of the wheelhorse of the Lomax family. And then there was Alan and Bess. Alan's the one that traveled with his father. He was that one that's exactly like him now, many of his personal characteristics, very much like old Lomax's. Lomax was such a delightful soul, you just would delight in his stories and accounts of people and this sort of thing, but he was this terrible conservative, see, at a time when liberalism was at its height, and during the Depression and New Deal.

Well, at any rate, Dobie became this very political guy, and he never hid his light under a bushel in terms of his opinion. He's let fly with some pretty strong opinions. And this came as a shock to a lot of the [people]. You understand World War II was building up, you know the whole international atmosphere was heating up considerably, and Hitler was moved in on Czechoslovakia, and Hitler was rampant,

and very threatening, and it was "Deutschland über alles." Well Dobie had, and I believe this quite honestly, with Dobie, he accused the Germans, for importing the concept of the Ph.D. The moving of dry bones from one graveyard to another, that was the exercise that he regarded as the whole Ph.D. program. Now Alan and I had become very close friends, and I was working on my bachelor and my master's, too. And Mody was. Well Mody and Dobie, Alan was in and out of town, but Mody and Dobie and Bedichek and Dr. Webb, he just listened, he never contributed folklore-wise, except that he had an ear, he leaned his ear over close and he heard Texas and the Plains talk. But he was a close friend of old Lomax's, too. And we'd spend half our time each time we'd get together, talking, telling Lomax stories about Mr. John A. because he was a character of the first water. Arbitrary, huffy, a great pouter if you hurt his feelings. In other words, if Mr. Lomax and I were sitting here having a conversation, and I said "I've got to go to the bathroom" and he was in the middle of relating something to me, I'd come back and I'd say "All right," and he'd say, "Never mind." I'd violated one of his rules of being utterly attentive to him. . . .

The upshot was that I hit on this idea because I had begun going out into the black churches and spending a lot of time in very seriously collecting, and Mody encouraged me, and Dobie. Dobie loved my stuff, would love to have me. Dobie knew what I was doing, see, I would embroider, see I didn't have a recording machine, so I would embroider the character. Dobie said "That's real relating now, Johnny," says, "nothing can be duller than Dr. Payne" (who belonged to the Texas Folklore Society, Leonidas W. Payne), "bless his heart, sittin' there talkin' about, old Payne sittin' there talkin' about some damn scrap that he picked up in Alabama somewhere. Bore you to death. It 'ud kill folklore. Kill an interest in it. Don't blame people for thinking it was silly study. Just like Stith Thompson." But he was commenting on the academicians' approach to folklore. When I started working on my master's, in 1939, well actually in '38, but I really started cutting into doing it, and then Rudolph Willard, as I said, I was taking graduate courses under him, became very influential. Rudolph had a recording machine, a huge damn thing, we'd take it out to these churches. And it was the first one any of these people had ever heard or seen. This was around Central Texas, the rural areas. Most of the blacks lived in agricultural areas at that time. They weren't in the urban centers as they are today. But I had a very keen ear for folksay, and a very considerable skill at reproducing the speech of various persons that I would interview. And Dobie, this was Dobie's great delight, he'd have me recite. "Tell about that fellow, Johnny, tell about that old boy you ran into out in so-and-so." And he took almost, as I say, a paternal interest. And I adored him, I absolutely adored old Dobie, because there was an integrity and decency about the man. He never said yes when he meant no. He had, he was the essence of undiplomatic behavior. Not in the same sense that, his was never a personal kind. John Lomax personalized his. If you hurt his feelings, or if you contradicted him, Dobie didn't mind if you contradicted him. He'd say, "Well, I think you're a damn fool, but I've been a damn fool often enough to know." And uh, he had a great capacity for affection, genuine affection. Mr. Lomax did too, that.

When we really all got active together, Lomax came down from Dallas, he was living in Dallas. And I'd written a piece for the Texas Folklore Society Publications sometime in '39. I don't remember what the piece was even, now, but I'd done it in dialect. And Lomax came down, wrote a letter, to me and Dobie: "That's the silliest thing in the world, he writes it like a buffoon. . . ." and he didn't spare the hosses any [laughs].

JM: [Laughs.]

JF: And he's right, he was absolutely right. What I was trying to do was write dialect.

JM: Now I can find that. . . .

JF: "Dat," I'd write that for, "dat" for "that." But I'd just written it really as a kind of, from, it wasn't an accurate piece and Lomax had a very great respect for accuracy. . . .

JM: He was mad because he thought the dialect spelling was inaccurate?

JF: Uh-hm. And that I'd done it too sloppily, that I hadn't really listened with the ear and I hadn't reproduced a piece of authentic folksay, was the position. Well at any rate, Alan and I had become close friends then, Lomax, and I was teaching at the university, I was a tutor at the university then.

Alan was always a very progressive thinker. I mean, he thought, you know, he had approached this material from a sociological and anthropological point of view. Alan has a magnificent mind, he has one of the best minds I've ever encountered. And was a great influence on me as far as starting my thinking along the lines of these are a people talking about the society they live in. And Alan is the first one that called my attention to the protest songs, the protest in the black spirituals, see. When I'd heard blacks sing, "Heb'n, heb'n, everybody talkin' 'bout heb'n ain't goin' there, Heb'n, Heb'n." Alan is the one that said "Don't you know what they're saying? They were singing to the white folks, old white marster and all that was going to church, talking about how he loved Jesus and all." They all had to be good to go to heaven. But they couldn't say it, and "Follow the Drinking Gourd" and all of the songs, Alan is the first one that analyzed and found that these were protest songs, many of them. It was the only means of safe protest there was, to voice any kind of protest. He's the first one that pointed out to me that when you met a black man you met literally two men, one that was confronting white man, and one that had his own life, his own set of, with his black friends, that was totally different. You know, and Negroes did not enjoy being called "niggers" or "nigras." The proper word was "Negro." Alan was the first one. Now I told Dobie about that. "Well, I think Alan's carrying that too far, now. Darkies know we think a lot of 'em. They know their friends." And, well, this was a great problem with Dobie, trying to learn to say "Negro." He'd ask, "Johnny, now how do you and Alan want me to say it? Ne-GROW?" [Laughs].

I was, you know, had started working on this thesis. And there was a Rosenwald

Foundation at that time, in 1940. Well, it's been a number of years, and they gave fellowships for work amongst the blacks of the South, for libraries, and that sort of thing. And my, they came up with a project, Dobie and Lomax came up with a project, for me to apply for a Rosenwald fellowship to collect black folksay, and mostly black folk music in their churches, you know, in their church services. Alan said the whole service has to be, is a work of art, and it follows a very carefully designed pattern, and it relates. Alan see, had approached it very intellectually, and understood that it

had its roots, its origins in Africa. Most Southerners that I knew, I was raised in a family that loved to go hear the colored folks sing and at our church we'd have a colored choir come over and pay 'em, I guess, five dollars to come over and sing. Sometimes they'd come for nothing. But they'd come and put on a concert of those old colored spirituals that were just so wonderful. And it was the, that was the cultural contact between black and white. It was quite acceptable to go listen to 'em sing because blacks were supposed to be the best singers in the world, see. God did give 'em

that, you'd have to say "God give 'em a good voice. You get half a dozen of 'em together you gonna have half a dozen cracker-jack singers." Well, uh, Alan, it was the first time I became conscious of segregation. I was raised by very civilized parents who had, who treated the black with respect and, but always as a different species of citizen. And this was the accepted social situation, you know. . . .

I got my master's in the summer, got my B.A. in the spring and my master's in the summer, there had been a great deal of interest and they talked about this Rosenwald fellowship. And I had become, kind of

"Dobie's boy" on campus. We were great friends. But it was beyond just the matter of folklore, we were also interested in politics. And Dobie began to be interested in the sociological aspects of the black situation, the social structure of our society. And being a very honest man, he believed the liberated mind was the only true god, and you searched, you searched, let your mind search the horizons for new ideas. So he, you know, this was a great gift that he had, because he wasn't inhibited by orthodoxy and, and cant, both of which he loathed. Nor was Alan Lomax. Nor was Bedichek or Mody. Webb was very much of a orthodox thinker. He would be described as a liberal. But as far as the folklore itself was concerned our interests went beyond just the matter of folksay and the pure folklore aspect of it. We began to see the whole picture. And this was a great revelation to me because I began to realize the kind of, the society I lived in. And for the first time questioned segregation. And Dobie questioned it. And especially in light of Hitler's anti-Semitic pronouncements. This was one of the charges against him, that he was mistreating the Jews over there. It was one of the uglier aspects—I'll have to say it never did alarm the American people greatly, it was [not] something that they got agitated over. It never took on the aspect of say, attitudes toward abolition before the Civil War. But was one of the charges against him. And Dobie saw it as, "Hell, he got all his laws from us, Texas law books." We had, you know, legalized segregation, I mean we had Jim Crow laws on all the books, where any social contact between the races was strictly forbidden, by law. You had to make provisions for their separate toilets, separate drinking places, separate seating places on public conveyances and whatnot. And so this, all of these attitudes were, all became part of our conversation.

I belonged to the Folklore Society and we still had our annual meetings where people would present papers on interesting nicknames in East Texas, and folk stories from so-and-so county, ghost dogs, and this sort of thing. I spoke, I'd preach Negro sermons, because I could do one up brown. And I was called on to speak before the various civic groups and study groups and that sort of thing. So this is how I got, I guess my basis for my becoming an entertainer.

Dobie was widely respected as a yarn-spinner and he'd travel all across Texas to speak before high schools and before women's study groups. But he began to mix politics into it and kinda' shook the hell out of these very conservative groups when he would go right to the heart of the matter. And he had very strong convictions on World War II that the Germans had Hitler, just despised Hitler. He and I were going to fight Hitler somehow. Well I'm one-eyed and he's too damn old, but he'd been in World War I and we actually combined our politics with folklore at that time.

Because by this time Alan and I had become very close and Alan was, understood so clearly the implications, he understood, Alan would explain to me the meaning of the prison system, black prison system, there were segregated prisons of course. That the reason the material he collected in these prisons were so pure, that it derived directly from the slaveocracy in the South, that all the conditions prevailed where the white man had power of life and death over these prisoners. At the same time we were collecting together. He, Alan was the major collector, I mean he was a master collector. He traveled tirelessly into some area where there was a good singer. He'd traveled the South, I hadn't, I mean all over the United States. I hadn't even been to the West Indies. He and his father had established the Folk Archives at the Library of Congress and had attracted a great deal of attention with their very extensive studies. I was never in that category, I was strictly on a East Texas and Louisiana and Arkansas level of collecting. My speciality was black folklore. And, oh I'd collect, run into good storytellers and set 'em down. But you see mine was never really folklore, I was more interested in the dramatic and the entertaining aspect of the stories that I would collect, and I was a good interviewer. I spoke the language and I had a great deal of success in forming a degree of rapport with the black and getting 'em to make statements and getting 'em to make observations on their lives that ordinarily they would never confide to a white man. As I say, they had this schizophrenic position. But if you could get around, behind that, and I collected a couple of slave. . . . See there were still ex-slaves, and old Lomax is the one that suggested it: "Johnny, they're still down there in the Brazos bottoms, you'll find folks that lived under slavery and you ought to get their stories. Get 'em to tell their stories." And I did that, I got quite remarkable, because see, a number of people had taken down their statements in longhand, but you never heard the real voice telling the story about "I mem' old Massa' when he went off and then he come back and all of us was called up from the quarter," and you know that kind of thing. The instruments they ate with, each child was given a big spoon, and never saw a fork or a knife in their lives, and they ate mush mostly and things they could dip out of a big community bowl. All of these, all of these enchanted me, these authentic stories. From infancy I'd loved to sit and listen to stories, I'd had a number of elderly relatives who'd gone up the trail and who lived on the frontier and could remember when there were still Indian raids. Well, I'd always been a sucker for this. To find five different variations on "Froggy Went A-Courtin'" in different counties in Alabama had about the same interest to me as Einstein theory did, I mean just left me absolutely cold. But the meat, juicy stories that were told was what got me. And this Dobie approved very highly. And he didn't mind that I deviated from fact and colored in, sketched in places that actually hadn't occurred, that made it a more listenable piece of work. Alan did. And Dobie says, "And read some of the stuff Alan's had transcribed. My god, you can't read it. Jelly Roll Morton might be the most interesting man in the world, but Alan just transcribing with all his 'ahs' and repetition, it's boring to read, Johnny. You do it your way. Least you'll have readers."

JM: Did you, was it in this period that J. Mason Brewer was also, did you know him?

JF: Yes. Yes. J. Mason was over here at Huston-Tillotson, and he'd come to Dobie with some stories. He considered J. Mason Brewer, well, his attitude toward him was, I would say, colored by his attitude toward blacks, when he first met J. Mason Brewer. But he encouraged him, oh god, he encouraged the daylights out of him, because he realized that J. Mason Brewer had sources that nobody else had, and J. Mason Brewer was pretty dedicated to him. But J. Mason Brewer had the unenviable situation of having to deal with the white world as a black man, and he had most of the attitudes of a, I mean most of the mannerisms of a polite, intelligent black man dealing with the whites. He never offended 'em, they were,

he was quite a remarkable guy I realize now, and he dealt with them the only way they could be, he could deal with this material. Because you must understand that in the public at large at this time, nobody would take J. Mason Brewer seriously, except somebody like Dobie and Mody Boatright. He was just, "Who cares what black these black stories, who in the hell cares, who could possibly. . . . There's an old nigger tellin' a story. And he goes down there in the Brazos bottoms and collects these nigger preacher stories and I don't know anybody, I can't imagine wastin' time like that." This was the general, I'm describing the general attitude. Dobie didn't have that attitude at all.

I never knew Mason Brewer well. Alan's position was that the only really, the only real sensible black man was the militant black. Well there weren't very many militant blacks in the South, because they didn't stay in the South long or they didn't stay militant long if they, if they were. And Alan said the black that cuts up each other, what's called a "bad nigger," you know that was a common expression, "Well, he's a 'bad nigger.' That old nigger's a good worker, he's a good worker, but he's a bad nigger, 'cause he get off down there at those damn bucket shops and get drunk and get in a fight, cut up, hell they go down there, to get him out, you willin' to get him out of jail every Monday mornin', pay his fine, he'll make you a good hand durin' the week." Alan said this, these are the only real "adjusteds." Because no black could adjust to the damn system they were compelled to live under. The most contemptible thing in black society at that time was what they called a "pimp," that was the word for the black that reported to the white establishment on troublemakers and any organizations and things that threatened the structure of the community. And the whole law enforcement system from Georgia right through Texas was dedicated to keeping the nigger in his place. Any white that had dealings with blacks other than master and servant dealings with them, was potential threats because the CIO had been organized, and the CIO didn't care whether you were nigger or white. "Organizing these

niggers, too." And there was literally a bounty on their damn head in most counties of the South, when a CIO organizer would come.

This was during the period, see, of World War II, when there was great ferment in this country going on behind the scenes, and it was a very dramatic period. It radicalized Dobie. Dobie and I went to see Dr. [Rainey], we were going to have some black singers come on, to Texas Folklore meeting, and the Texas Folklore meeting was going to be held at the University of Texas on the campus. And Dobie and I talked with Dr. Rainey who was president of the university and a great friend of ours, very, very intelligent man, who felt as we did about blacks, but Dobie said, "If we announce it, announce, go around and get permission, Johnny, we'll never get it, they haven't got any choice but to say 'No.' If we just go ahead and do it, hell, we'll put 'em on a show. You get up there and run the thing, and we'll put 'em on a show that they'll know nobody's going to raise any thunder about it except a few jackasses and we won't pay any attention to them." And so we did, and about a year later, we went to Dr. Rainey, because by this time I, I'd known a great number of Negro educators. J. Mason Brewer never fell into this category, but a number of blacks out here at Huston-Tillotson, you know, were starting to rumble and mumble about "We got to change things up." And they wanted to come to the Fine Arts School, put on concerts at Hogg Memorial Auditorium on Sunday afternoon, various pianists, student string quartets and whatnot, singers. And uh, this was in '42, '43. Had to be in '42 because I went off in '43, and I was gone from '43 on.

Well, the blacks had asked us, said, "Look, why can't we come to that, we'll sit up in the balcony," they were perfectly willing to sit up in the balcony, although I'd say there never was an audience over forty people came to these damn concerts, they were mostly faculty exercises, see. And "we love to be able to do this," and certainly the artists were perfectly willing, most of these, you know the faculty, all faculty artists, some of them with national reputations, here. And they were very happy, and said

"By all means, we'd welcome a black audience, in fact we think it's a disgrace there's not one, they're not admitted." And we went in to see Dr. Rainey, and made the pitch, can't we on Sunday afternoon without any fanfare or anything just have this group, there never would be over eight or nine of them, maybe a dozen at the outside and they'd sit politely up in the segregated section. And by this time they were after Rainey's hide, the Board of Regents were, and one of the charges against him was "he advocates niggers and white people going to school together." And the only black that was allowed on the campus then was, had to be carrying a package, had to be there on a mission. And he said, "I'll have to tell you it would be just what they would hope would go on, and spread it all over Texas about 'niggers up there, sitting there with white folks listening.'" Well Dobie was impatient with that, I wasn't, I said "I understand," because this would be used; Dobie felt, "Well the hell with 'em, son-of-a-bitches," as Dobie said, "the Board of Regents cares as much about the true function of a university in the community as a razorback boar in East Texas cares about Keats's 'Ode on a Grecian Urn.'" I cite that instance to give you an idea of the kind of tensions that were arising.

And I had already become so moved, see, I was in great demand as a speaker, I was a very entertaining speaker, and I could do these, uh, I'd recorded a great deal then because I was on a fellowship, I'd gotten a grant, and I'd collected some rare and beautiful church services and sermons, just breathtaking. So I was in great demand as a speaker and I'd bring along my recording machine, play it to civic clubs and that sort of thing, but I'd always throw in, you know, "Well, we're embattled in a life-and-death struggle with fascism, and with Hitler and Hirohito. And it would behoove us to give thought to what we're doing to a segment of our society, we're going to have to rethink our position." Well this was just terribly offensive to [some people].

Then I Dobie and I were going to go see if we couldn't get in the merchant marine. Because see I'd been. . . .

JM: Dobie wanted to go in the merchant marine, too?

JF: Yes, he wanted to get where the action was, wanted to go off and fight. So I went down to Galveston, and he was too old, he wasn't qualified, but they took me. And I went on a tanker in 1942. I'd had my fellowship grant granted me for another year, but I suspended that and I quit teaching at the university and I went into the merchant marine, sailing high-test gasoline over to England. And Dobie by this time had become quite wrapped up in my affairs, my career. I took great notes, by this time I'd learned to be a great note-taker and we got torpedoed over in the Irish Sea, not seriously, but the boat had to be laid up in Avonmouth, and Dobie was an Anglophile, he thought England was standing firm against the Hitler menace. Which they, indeed they were, and he was a great champion of the Soviet Union. "Hitler's bit off a chunk," he told me when Stalin declared war . . . "that he won't digest." He said, "these knownothings, goddammit, they better, instead facing what the damn Russians really a people and maybe got a different society but they're a people, and Hitler's gonna wish he hadn't of gone that direction." You know, up until that time, '41, when Hitler declared war on Russia, Hitler hadn't been defeated. He just marched over the map of Europe with his iron heel and France had fallen in '40, and there was great ferment in the country over, and Hitler of course was swung down through North Africa heading to join up with the Japanese, and they'd have the globe encircled. And this was their master plan. We had entered the war by then, but as I say, I was disqualified, and Dobie was disqualified from service, and we were both very anxious to get in the fray, and that's how the merchant marine thing came about.

But the Rockefeller Foundation had taken a great interest in me by then, and Henry Nash Smith, incidentally, was teaching at the university then, and he was part of the, our group that would go out to either Dobie's ranch or to Webb's ranch and sit all night long and talk, tell Lomax stories. The Lomax stories were our favorite thing, old man, about old man Lomax. "I remember when he did so-and-so and so-and-so." And uh, Lomax and Bedichek had had great exchange of letters, they were

both great letter writers, and delightful ones. Dobie had become really radicalized by then. And when I say radicalized, he'd began, I'm using it in its true sense, he'd gone to the root. He saw racism as a genuine injustice and also a threat to all the ideas that we proclaimed from the housetops to be the principles and ideals upon which this republic was founded. He never lost his capacity to understand the thinking of the people that he had come from, but he understood why they felt that way, that it was their inheritance. And he, he didn't share my feelings, that well, all you have to do is tell these folks that they're wrong and they'll correct their thinking right away and it'll accord with yours in the future.

Now, I've given you kind of a rough picture, every time I'd come back, when I went off in the merchant marine. Dobie gloried in it, Henry Nash Smith and others. There was a wonderful guy, Dr. David Stephens, who was head of the humanities division of the Rockefeller Foundation that was talking about giving me a Rockefeller grant to really, really do some serious work with the black field. I stopped in to see him when I was in New York, with my ship, my ship was anchored up in the Hudson, and I went up, he lived in Upper Montclair. And he said, "There's an organization, the Red Cross has a service, a overseas service, that they are looking for young men. And Johnny, you, any man that's been through high school can work on a ship, I think you could make better use of your talents and your abilities if you went into the field service, overseas field service with the Red Cross." And he investigated and I applied and that's how I went over to the Middle East, for a year. Dobie and I corresponding the whole time. Dobie had gone off to Cambridge by this time. And Lomax, Alan, was in the Signal Corps, which was kind of the communications department. Alan had gone to New York, sold CBS on the idea of doing a program called "Back Where I Come From," and Alan had discovered Burl Ives and Woody Guthrie and Josh White. He had an absolute genius for discovering remarkable talent. And, to the public as a whole there was no vogue in folk music whatever, it was regarded as really beneath serious consideration by the public. It had no, it had no audience save in colleges. And Bess by this time, in true Lomax fashion, had become a serious musicologist and she had gone to [New York], she and Alan were the liberated minds of the family. . . .

But Alan and I remained very close friends. I was not as well informed politically.

But, I had a very great understanding, and Dobie understood, too, and we had very strong political opinions, and I did. Our trouble, Dobie and I got into trouble, mostly, because of our attitude toward the black. We had pretty much arrived at the same time that it was an injustice for the black to be forcibly denied full educational opportunities, full capacities as human beings. J. Mason Brewer understood that very well, but he never got out on that limb at all, this never inspired him. But inspired a lot of young blacks that I'd meet down at Prairie View College and whatnot, because they were already radicalized. But I came back in '44 from the Middle East, and they took me under limited service into the Army, and I was stationed out to Camp Swift, Texas, which was not, of course, right in the heat throb of the battle field. So about every two weeks I'd be up here and spend the evening with Dobie and Bedichek and Henry Nash Smith, Mody and Webb out at either Webb's place. . . .

*A corral on the SMS ranch near Spur, Texas, May 1939. (LC-USF33-12213-M3) Photograph by Russell Lee. Farm Security Administration Collection, Library of Congress*

JM: Was Bill Owens around here then?

JF: No. He wasn't here. He was in and out. Bill and I knew each other, but Bill's approach was quite different from ours. He was a pure folklorist. He, I would say a very conservative gentleman, and we were all of us, you know, about a lot of things besides folklore. Bedichek loved Bill Owens and, because Bill had been raised in East Texas. But Bill was really a very serious collector and a tedious collector, I could never bring myself to the kind of really studious approach that he gave to folklore, collecting these songs. I remember a song that became a great popular hit called [sings]: "A Tiskit, A Tasket, I lost my yellow basket, dada, dada, dada, dada, . . . ." And Bill did a piece on this, on the origins of this, where, where this had really come from, that it wasn't a Hollywood, Tin Pan Alley song at all, that it was an old folk, children's play-song. And this is the kind of thing that Bill did excellently. But my interest was on a, not nearly so academic a level. And Dobie, I would say, combined the academic and the kind of more general, humane, I mean human aspects of folklore.

JM: Let me sidetrack you just a second, since you mention that. I know you're in the middle of something about Dobie and so on during the war, but since you mention it, did the political interests of yourself and

Dobie and company synchronize or not synchronize with the more academically oriented kind of folklore? Actually there were academicians on both sides of the political camp, because Alan Lomax was very much, he could be very academic about the folklore.

JF: Oh, oh yes.

JM: Was there ever any sense, though, that the academic pursuit of folklore in tedious detail was supportive of political conservatism in any way, or political liberalism?

JF: No, it would lead you the other direction. After all, that's what had happened to me, I'd become politicized by my work in folklore as had Alan Lomax. His father never had. See, his father never, didn't have time to, he was very, very, very paternal toward the black. But he wouldn't hesitate to give one a dime to sing all day for him. Alan was very sensitive to that kind of thing and Dobie was. Of course Dobie never collected any with machines, never went for it like that. Most of his, most of his collecting had been done with *corridos*, folk stories from South Texas in Spanish and translating it to English. He loved the poetry of these

people, poetry of the earth. See, it was Dobie's strong contention that we had created an art form that was indigenous to Texas and this is where our strength lay, by turning our eyes back this direction. This was his great influence on me, taking a pride in the fact that we did come from the earth and contended with the frontier. And he had no use for the Hollywood cowboy, the cowboy that Dobie idealized—he didn't idealize him. They were working people, they didn't carry guns and didn't have gunfights. They carried . . . his uncle Jim had been a cattleman all his life and he had a .44 pistol that he'd never shot in his entire life. Somebody'd given it to him or he'd bought it on impulse sometime early in life. It stayed in his drawer until it got to where it wouldn't shoot as far as Dobie knew. And none of the cattlemen that he ever interviewed were gunslingers or, and this was purely the creation of the pulp magazine people and romantic writers. They were showoffs; Tom Mix and Hoot Gibson were their ideal. Had very little to do with the day-to-day working situation on the range. And, of course, Lomax, this was Lomax's approach, too. There was nothing whatever

colorful and joyous about working cattle, putting up with sick cows, doctoring sick calves and you know, it was backbreaking work. There was a certain nobility about it, because these people that had an integrity, Dobie had a great deal of respect for their integrity, knew there were drunks and deadbeats amongst them, but he had very little use for the showmanship, he had no use at all for a rodeo, for instance. Thought it made a lot of sense for the Mexican vaquero who had no other form of entertainment for them all to get together on a ranch and demonstrate their roping and riding skills, but as far as bulldogging and bronco riding, the object was to get a horse and break him from throwing you, not to try to value him for his ability to throw you off, he wasn't any good as a work animal. Dobie's was a very realistic approach to the ranching industry. He loved horses, he loved the range, and he loved the people that worked it and made their living from it. But he didn't, his stories, all the stories he collected were the stories that dealt with the life and the working conditions of these people and the accurate account of who

these people really were and what they had to contend with. How they held on with their backs to the wall and this sort of thing. How you could trust a man that said "I'll deliver you 500 400-lb. yearlin's, steers, next spring," would do it, or pay. His word was all, nothing was written down. Dobie valued this very highly as the way a society should operate, where there was mutual trust, mutual understanding. And inviolable laws that you couldn't, that were unalterable as far as human conduct. He had a great respect for integrity and held it in very high regard. Dobie was one of the most honest human beings I ever encountered. Absolute integrity.

So did Alan Lomax, incidentally. And I would say old man Lomax within his limitations did. But he never had the expansive mind that Dobie did. Oh, he'd despair of Dobie. Dobie wrote a article, he had a column that several Texas papers wrote and in 1941 he wrote this column on Pappy O'Daniels. Dobie'd gone down to speak at the San Jacinto Monument on San Jacinto Day, and Pappy O'Daniels had come sweeping in there, he was governor of Texas, had come sweeping in there unannounced. His whole coterie of followers and announced that he was going to give the address, he had a very important address to give and they had to change the whole program to accommodate the governor of Texas. And it was purely a political move because Pappy O'Daniels wanted to announce that one of the senators, a junior senator from Texas, Shepard, had died and Dobie wanted to announce that, rather, Pappy wanted to announce that he was appointing his successor. And so Pappy O'Daniels takes over the stage out there, the proceedings. And Dobie goes storming around and stomping around inside the damn monument because he don't want to hear the son-of-a-bitch. And he got back in time, it was a rainy day, and got back in time, the skies parted just before the ceremony started and Pappy O'Daniels got up and said "Old Sam Houston, smiling down from heaven, the Almighty has parted the clouds to hear, to see because he knew that I was going to announce that his last remaining son, General Robert E. Lee, or General Thomas Jefferson Houston, has been appointed to the United States Senate." The old gentleman was eighty-odd years old and was senile and also bedridden, and Dobie was so outraged by this announcement, its what he regarded as an absolute desecration of San Jacinto Day and the whole thing, he wrote this column and ended up as as, Pappy had written a song that had become that had kind of become a theme song of Texas, [sings] "Beautiful, beautiful Texas, the state where the bluebonnets grow / The land where our forefathers, died at the Alamo." And old Dobie quotes a passage because Pappy led the whole congregation in singing. And Dobie described it with just a bitter, savage pen, and it ended up, "Oh beautiful, beautiful Texas, land where our forefathers died, Oh beautiful puppy vomit, Oh beautiful buzzard puke." And that was the end of his column. Well old Lomax, I was gonna drive him around, I'd drive Lomax a lot when he'd come to Austin, come down from Dallas, and he greeted me at the Alamo Hotel, with that paper, just shaking all over. "Frank can't do this, this is disgraceful, he's gonna wreck his reputation writing trash like this. I can't stand O'Daniels either, but you don't write this for the public to view. Beautiful puppy vomit, beautiful buzzard puke. Those words don't appear in family newspapers." And Dobie just laughed, it bothered Dobie not a bit. He was very fond of Mr. Lomax, as I was, of Mr. Lomax's idiosyncracies and his posturing would become, were the source of just endless anecdotes for us. Dobie would, just reveled in them, and Bedichek did, and Mody would always smile his gentle smile. Mody was a very gentle man, you know. . . .

JM: Okay, well, this is a story from Shirley [Lomax].

JF: Yeah, Shirley was telling it. Bess was just a—not even a teenager then, and driving along and Lomax talking away to her and there's a car in front of them and Lomax speeded up and kept honking at the man; just h-o-n-king, just sittin' on the horn. And the guy, there was plenty of room for Lomax to go around. Lomax wanted him to remove his vehicle from this pathway and the fellow finally just pulled over and was glaring and Lomax drove se-

dately on past and then dropped back down to his 30 miles. (laughter) And the guy behind him! And Shirley said Bess came in in tears, she was crying, said she frequently was from her father's beratings. Bess couldn't restrain commenting on the fact: now you honk the man out of the way, now you're driving slower than he was driving! Lomax refused to speak to her. These kind of anecdotes, these are what we would spend whole evenings telling, Lomax stories to one another. Dobie, Bedichek, Webb, and Mody. And Mody was always just a listener.

JM: Did any of this kind of thing happen at the Folklore Society meetings?

JF: I don't recall ever any kind of fracas at Folklore Societies. They weren't the kind of people that got into fracases.

JM: Can we go back a little bit. . . .

JF: You have to understand that Lomax regarded himself as genuinely the father—the originator—of it all here in Texas, so he not only assumed the mantle, but he acted the part. And wasn't condescending, but he was always very mindful of that fact and you were damn well conscious of it, any matter regarding folklore, collection of folklore. Lomax was terribly offended at Leadbelly. Because he got Leadbelly out of the penitentiary. Leadbelly was a chauffeur and also gave them all their songs. Well Alan, by this time is in his thirties. Alan had become very conscious of the fact, you know, the black was the last man—sat on the last row and came through the back door. Lomax accepted that and he defended that system. And he was a Mississippian and was of the Southern gentry; regarded himself as Southern gentry and they weren't Southern gentry, but he regarded himself as part of the Southern gentry and supported the system. And Leadbelly got uppity one time and threatened Mr. Lomax's life. Scared the hell out of Alan cause he knew by this time they'd grown up a kind of a rapport and Alan was very defensive of Leadbelly; Alan's one that related the incident to me. But it was quite a frightening experience. And Lomax never forgave Leadbelly for that. It wasn't the way you treated your benefactor. You didn't speak to him like that.

JM: Did Lomax ever talk about his experiences when he was a boy . . . ?

JF: Yes, they were always idealized. He had a sister here.

JM: . . . like a story about Nat, his boyhood friend that he talks on?

JF: Yes, yes. But they—Lomax idealized his background a great deal. Nothing comes to mind right now. . . . But Lomax—and I could be wrong about this—but Lomax was never capable of breaking the cultural straitjacket in terms of the separation, segregation of the races and his was a very fraternal, familial attitude towards blacks. But part of his family is very sweet and that, but he would say things that to a black militant today would send him scatty. And would send Alan scatty. And Alan and he would get in terrible fights.

JM: Well, how did he come to do this thing? Why did he collect black folklore?

JF: Because Lomax had—Lomax was unquestionably a genius. He is a man of a magnificent mind [but] he never put the two and two together. He never questioned the system. That this was then—that lynching was the inevitable result of such a system. That it was a method by which—and while he disapproved of it very profoundly—I would, this is the way I would analyze the situation. He'll never say, "Well the system itself creates this." He would just say, "These are aberrations of lawless people." And he would never approve an injustice, an overinjustice to a black. On the contrary, he wouldn't—you just didn't do it any more than my mother would. My mother accepted segregation. Had to the first part of her life until we all became pretty active integrationist in the late forties and early fifties. And my father always was and—but never an activist. He was a lawyer and tried their cases for them and was much respected by the whole black community. But he didn't actively; he said that time would have to take care of that, but his daddy's position always was. Daddy was politically a very, very aware man. But Daddy's position was that so long as white man's place is up here and the blacks down there, that's all well and good. But when the black decided his place was up here, too, it was going to be a day of reckoning in our soci-

ety. And that day was surely coming. And Lomax, I don't think, ever felt that this system would change or should change. He regarded the black as—he accepted the political and social strictures of our society. Alan didn't; Dobie and I didn't after the forties.

I got my FBI file here a couple of years ago. And I was in it. I didn't think I was in the FBI, but I was in it. And the fascinating thing about the file was, that this is where they picked me and Dobie up. This is where we first—our names first got in in 1943, I think. Faulk has been inducted into the Communist party by Frank Dobie. This is all trash and mishmash that goes into file. These are just the reports special agents get from informers. And it's a far graver, an outrageous reflection on the misuse of power by a government agency than it is any—it is also a comment on the political climate of the day. We—what was it—oh, that's right, we belong and we're very outspoken in an organization called "National Committee to Abolish the Poll Tax." In the opinion of the FBI, that was obviously a communist-inspired thing.

JM: Nobody ever tried to include the Texas Folklore Society as some kind of communist-inspired outfit, because of Dobie?

JF: Oh, heavens, no, never. But folksong itself was under attack during the McCarthy period. As were folk singers that sing these songs, call 'em "protest songs." This went before that House on Un-American Activities Committee and this sort of thing. They were after mostly Woody Guthrie and Pete Seeger, who were very outspoken in their political views, Woody was, you know, not only would proclaim his membership in the Communist party but defended it. And that's when folklore came under attack. All folk music. Alan used to tell me in the thirties that one day all America would be singing their own songs. They'd understand the richness and the importance of their own folk culture. Alan was—this was one of his great theses in the twenties. I would say that was shared by his father. But the importance, Lomax placed great importance, John A., placed great importance on this. As a matter of

fact, he was kind of the discoverer of this fact. That this is where the real poetry of the people is. It wasn't until, see, the fifties until a group called the Weavers, Pete Seeger and three others, I've forgotten their names now, sang these songs. "Goodnight, Irene," for instance, was our theme song—always—when I was with Alan and he'd always end up the evening by "Let's all sing it" when I'd be in New York with them. Leadbelly the "King of the Twelve String" would lead the singing; that was his song, and Alan had copyrighted it for him. Well, when this burst on the American scene, the radio, it became a great smash hit. This was the whole beginning of the popularization of folk music. And Alan went off to Europe collecting. Had a profound influence on the BBC, as you know, you got all the stars searching out British folk music. Started people singing there, and then went to Italy and collected, and Spain and collected, and

France and collected. He was better known over there than he was here. He was away eight years, from 1949 to 1958 over there collecting. And because this was the McCarthy period and folk music was under attack; he was certainly under attack. He, my God, early on he was under attack. Because he brought the whole folk singing to the CBS, but it had been just an esoteric public service show, it had never had any sponsorship, but he collected jazz musicians from down in New Orleans and as I say, Burl Ives, Woody Guthrie, and promoted and worked tirelessly with them. Progressives had begun to attach a lot of importance to it, but it was confined entirely to that. I think that Woody Guthrie and Peter Seeger that first started hootenannies when they were singing at concerts in Washington, I mean in New York and that sort of thing. And there was a stirring of interest in it and folk music, but it was only when the Weavers made this smash hit and it swept the country, "Sanna, Sanna, Sanna" which is an Israeli song and "Goodnight, Irene" that it swept. And then while Alan was in Europe, the enterprising Tin Pan Alley men went down to Washington, all this stuff went to the Library [of Congress], and got all "On Top of Old Smokey" and all the folk songs that Alan had collected, all of them. Changed them up enough and copyrighted themselves and there broke out a great rash during the fifties of folk music that rose to its heights in the sixties, you see, where every kid had a guitar and they were all doing just what Alan said every summer camp. You know, it became the rage. Alan came back in '58 and discovered all of the music that he'd collected and persons from whom he'd collected, their names weren't even on. And this, oh God, he stayed with me. I was in New York and he lived at my place. Just went into a tailspin. And it was just by the nearest fluke that he had copyrighted "Goodnight, Irene" in Leadbelly's name. And Leadbelly's estate reaped the benefits.

JM: I wasn't aware of that.

JF: Leadbelly—"Goodnight, Irene" was a combination of about a dozen different snatches. Leadbelly was good at creating that kind of thing. He'd hear it one way and you know, if you sing the whole song through, it doesn't make a damn bit of sense.

JM: You've met him and heard him sing while . . .

JF: Oh, yeah. He stayed with me in New York. Leadbelly lived near me. Leadbelly and I were very close friends. Woody Guthrie lived with me. Alan is the one that got me to come to New York. He sold CBS on taking me on as a great—you see, Alan was very much like his father in that respect. I was the best in the business. I could delineate Southern character better than anybody in the world. And there was no exception to that from Alan's point of view. And, as you see, Alan's early collecting, people that lived with him and he cared for, that he looked after, when folklore became great vogue everywhere, the word went out that Lomax was nothing more than exploiter of these

poor, hard working people. This was a cruel and vicious thing to say, because Alan had been literally, not only their benefactor, but their discoverer.

JM: Well, there seems to be an unavoidable political connection.

JF: No, my interest—folklore led me into really an understanding of the fabric of this society. And injustices that had to be corrected. That's the reason I early on became an advocate of attacking racism in this country. I consider it a very, very grave disease that we're going to have to address head-on. We can't leave it for another generation and another generation.

JM: Really, the puzzle is still John A. because he does the seminal work. He's got the idea to go do this stuff; to collect from these people. Or at least he's the one that really carries the bat.

JF: And he's the best I ever met at doing

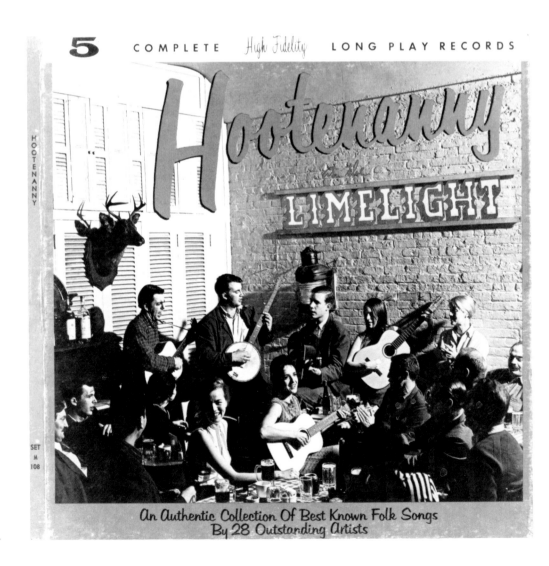

*In the 1960s the "Weavers" and other entertainers inspired a generation of college students to take up guitar and banjo and to patronize the coffeehouses that sprang up near every campus. Some formed groups of their own, like Colgate University friends Dan Adams and Gerry Parsons, who performed under the name "Dan and the Deacon" and are pictured here (center, with banjo and guitar) at the Limelight Cafe in New York's Greenwich Village. Photograph by George Pickow. Album cover courtesy of James Hardin*

it. He could find them, what he was looking for, and was tireless in his energies in searching out for folk artists of America.

JM: But, his political opinions get, if anything, more rigid.

JF: Yes, I think so in his old age. Well, you see, he was in banking and finance and he was surrounded . . . his companions there, I mean, his associates there were very conservative men, and presumably, their attitudes, their rationalizations for the way the system worked so that they could scrape, draw off the cream from on top. With those that he accepted too; he never challenged that. He was an artist and a thinker, but not a thinker on that level. Alan early on did, Alan during the thirties did. And presumably the more deeply Alan delves, the more the whole truth was revealed. And long before it was to me and to Dobie. Dobie and I arrived about the same time, in fact that racism was racism and it was a myth that must be attacked. It was a myth. It must release the potential of the people, or otherwise it could destroy us. And, you see, Dobie was an honest man who, as I say, exercises the true function of a radical, namely to go to the root of the problem. And he began to understand the political and the economic implications of racism and I would say he and I did it together but never with the profundity that Alan did. We were never, never with the scholarliness Alan brought to it. You know Alan has a, as I say, a very comprehensive mind. You know, it all fits together. Dobie had a slightly impulsive pattern of behavior, you know, he would plunge into a subject and, as he said, "My God, Johnny, hell I never would debate on one of these radio shows, television shows. I might discuss some, but I never debated. Hell, I'm not a debater and I'm not gonna have that kind of mind. I'm not like Alan. Alan examines and comprehends all the ramifications of the positions he takes on."

I was going to say about Dobie something that Dobie and I discussed a number of times; the implications of folklore and once you get into that, you have to understand what it really is all about, it's about people. And this had a great expanding effect on Dobie's whole political and social philosophy. And, just as it did mine. And consequently when the McCarthy period came along, we were outraged by it. Dobie never had any use for Communists. I don't mean by that that he said, "Get that guy away." You know, hell, Dobie—they were like foot-washing Baptists to Dobie. They were an esoteric group that had the truth, and any deviations from their particular brand of truth was not permitted. They were orthodox and Dobie had no use for orthodoxy. He felt it was a confining thing, just as I did. That's the reason neither of us—that's what makes it so damn funny. But on the other hand, he never had any desire of punishing any of them. He felt that this was all a stalking horse, just as I did, the whole communistic conspiracy idea. And this was shared by, of course, Alan and it was certainly shared by Bedichek and Mody Boatright. But not to be anti-Communist, you know, and not to go along of the idea of, "well, by God, it should not be only be deprived of their civil rights, but should be treated as a threat to our society," which we never conceived the Communist party to be in this country because they had no . . . Dobie'd say, "Hell, Johnny, they couldn't elect a damn man county commissioner in any part of the United States, what in the hell is this . . . this is your hypocrites. See, the damn people in Houston, Dallas, damn bankers, big insurance men, going around talking about your Yankees are coming down here, stirring up our darkies. Same damn technique is to hide the true meaning of what these perpetrators of this damned evil system on us are. I'm not turning into a damn Communist. Hell, I don't know but three or four of them. Some of them good people, honest people. But hell, I know good Catholics, and I know good Baptists. Don't share their damned opinions, but I don't believe in persecuting them. [laughter] I don't believe they should be denied any rights that I want to enjoy myself." Well, this was very basic to Dobie's philosophy which I regard as good, solid understanding of what this republic is all about. And very strong convictions, and I share them, most of them. All of which derive from our early folklore experiences in America.

# Ethnic Heritage and Language Schools

## Introduction

"Ethnic schools" may be a vague and somewhat mystifying classification for most Americans. Yet nearly everyone knows someone who attended an after-school, weekend, or all-day program called "Hebrew School," "Lithuanian School," "Polish School," "Japanese School," or the like. Such schools are organized by ethnic communities as a supplement to the educational requirements that ordinary public and private schools are designed to meet. But there is virtually no awareness of ethnic schools as a national phenomenon.

Over the past two decades, as educationists and the public were drawn into a long, fractious, and still unresolved debate about bilingual education, no one referred to the widespread and longstanding use of ethnic schools by hundreds of American ethnic communities. The experience of ethnic schools may or may not be a helpful model for bilingual education; but so far as we at the American Folklife Center could determine, only one scholar has undertaken pro-

longed and serious research at the national level regarding ethnic schools—sociolinguist Joshua Fishman of Yeshiva University.

To begin remedying that inattention, the American Folklife Center in 1982 launched the Ethnic Heritage and Language Schools Project. The project secured the services of a number of researchers around the country to visit, document, and analyze an ethnic school in their vicinity. Research locations were chosen to give a diverse sampling: different ethnic groups, different regions of the country, and different kinds of schools. The list below shows which schools were visited by project workers.

Armenian, Watertown, Massachusetts
Cambodian, Houston, Texas
Chinese, San Antonio, Texas
Czech, Cedar Rapids, Iowa
Dutch, Pella, Iowa
German-Russian, Strasburg, North Dakota
Greek, Birmingham, Alabama
Greek, Buffalo, New York
Hebrew, Nashville, Tennessee
Hungarian, New Brunswick, New Jersey
Hupa Indian, Hoopa Valley, California
Islamic, Seattle, Washington
Japanese, Los Angeles, California
Korean, Silver Spring, Maryland
Latvian, Milwaukee, Wisconsin
Lebanese, Birmingham, Alabama
Polish, Chicago, Illinois
Portuguese, Taunton, Massachusetts
Turkish, New York, New York
Ukrainian, Woonsocket, Rhode Island

Those who would delve into the project in more detail can read its final report, *Ethnic Heritage and Language Schools in America*, Studies in American Folklife, number 4, which includes an introduction by project coordinator Elena Bradunas, essays by thirteen of the project workers describing the schools they visited, and photographs from many of the schools. Four of the essays are excerpted here to share with readers of *Folklife Annual* some of our glimpse into ethnic schools in America.

AJ

# The First Korean School
# Silver Spring, Maryland

BY LUCY M. LONG

In 1982 an estimated six hundred thousand Koreans and Korean-Americans were living in the United States, congregated in three major population centers: Los Angeles (with about two hundred thousand Korean residents), Chicago, and New York. San Francisco and Washington, D.C., have the next largest Korean populations. The Korean Embassy estimates that between thirty-five and forty thousand Koreans live in the Washington metropolitan area, the locale of the First Korean School.

The majority of the Korean population in the United States arrived within the last thirty years. The Washington, D.C., population is even more recent—only fifteen to twenty years old. The first generation of Koreans born in America is now coming of age, and the problems they face are new ones for the Korean community.

Many Koreans come to the United States for occupational or educational reasons, some to escape what they feel is an overly competitive and restrictive society in Korea, and others to provide their children with opportunities they might not have in their homeland. Many give up established careers, social status, and economic security, and their first years here are often a struggle for survival, full of long hours at low-paying jobs. Even so, most Korean immigrants succeed financially in the United States, often achieving economic stability within five or ten years. Many of them own their homes and businesses and send their children to the best schools and colleges.

Korean history, which extends back five thousand years, has included a continuous struggle to maintain an identity distinct from that of Japan and China. The small country has nurtured many scholars, artists, and inventors. A respect for tradition and the past, which is reinforced by the contemporary achievements of Koreans, is an integral part of Korean culture. On the whole, Koreans living in the United States have retained their cultural pride; they maintain a distinctive personal ethnic identity

and express a community identity through numerous ethnic organizations.

Christian churches, particularly Presbyterian and Baptist, function as the central social organization in many Korean communities. Washington, D.C., has over sixty Korean churches, many of which have their own buildings. They offer a variety of services to the Korean community, including Korean language classes for children. Approximately twelve Washington-area churches sponsor such classes.

The First Korean School was established on June 5, 1977, by the First Korean Baptist Church of Silver Spring, Maryland. The school became an incorporated institution within the state of Maryland separate from the church on April 10, 1979. As of spring 1982, it maintained relations with the church, but is growing increasingly independent in financial and policy matters. It is also growing in size and reputation.

The school is located in Silver Spring, Maryland, in the annex and basement classrooms of the First Korean Baptist Church. Situated on Georgia Avenue, five miles beyond the Washington, D.C., beltway, the church is surrounded by Maryland suburbs. Korean lettering on a sign in front of the building is the only indication of the church's ethnic identity.

Over 150 kindergarten, elementary, junior high, and high school students attend the First Korean School. A faculty of thirteen teachers and two administrators teach the classes in Korean language, music, dance, and martial arts. The primary emphasis is on Korean language (both reading and speaking), but other subjects are included to attract the children's interest and to expose them to Korean culture and values.

Classes meet every Saturday from 9:30 A.M. to 1:00 P.M. and follow the American public school calendar, with summer and winter vacations. The school celebrates most American holidays, as well as selected Korean ones. Students enroll by semester

*Above: In music class, April 24, 1982. (195616-5--12) Photograph by Carl Fleischhauer*

*Right: Martial arts class instructed by Mr. Myung Chul Choi, April 17, 1982. (193186-1-19A) Photograph by Lucy Long*

and receive report cards and certificates of achievement at the end of the school year.

Although the school is nominally independent of the church in which its classes are held, members of the First Korean Baptist Church play important roles in the school's administration. The church also provides classroom space and utilities, but in all other ways the school is self-supporting, earning funds for faculty salaries and supplies from the students' tuition fees.

The First Korean School was created by a small group of Korean immigrants living in the Maryland suburbs of Washington, D.C. Mr. Han il Lee, the current principal, initiated the idea and spearheaded the organization of the school, aided by church and community leaders.

Before starting the school, Mr. Lee sought advice from a number of persons involved in ethnic language education. The Washington Korean School, created in 1970, the oldest Korean school in the Washington metropolitan area, provided an example of an established school. The Korean Embassy's Office of Education, which works with Korean ethnic schools throughout the country, supplied other models, as well as official support and a representative to the school board. Mr. Lee also drew ideas from other ethnic communities—specifically, Finnish, Polish, Jewish, Chinese, and Japanese—and their organizations.

Mr. Lee also organized the original financing of the school. He obtained approximately one-third of the funds for supplies and administrative expenses from the First Korean Baptist Church, which considered this aid to be part of its Christian service to the Korean community. The rest was paid for by students' tuitions. The church also provided free use of its facilities and utilities.

While the First Korean School identifies itself as a language school for teaching the "mother tongue" to Korean descendents, its administrators state that its primary purpose is to create good Korean-American citizens. They believe that the more a child understands and appreciates his ethnic heritage, the better person he will become and the more smoothly his acculturation into American society will be accomplished. By giving him the opportunity to know his background, the school provides the child with more options to choose from when he begins to develop his own perspective on his ethnic identity. These goals can best be accomplished by teaching the Korean language, using it as a vehicle for transmitting Korean values and beliefs, as well as by teaching about Korean culture and history.

Facilitating communication between generations is another major concern of the Korean School. Language is often a barrier between parents and children, particularly since many Korean families are recent immigrants. Because of their interaction with native-born English-speakers through their schooling, the children usually learn English within a few years of their arrival,

*Special class students holding signs that tell their plans for summer vacation, June 19, 1982. (198070-1-12) Photograph by Lucy Long*

School principal Mr. Han il Lee points to words on a chart as students sing, April 24, 1982. (195616-3-30) Photograph by Carl Fleischhauer

while the parents take much longer. Often parents and grandparents never become fluent in the language and speak Korean among themselves and in their homes. As Mr. Noh, the sixth grade teacher and a board member. says:

Their mother tongue, Korean, is needed as a tool of communication between generations. Sometimes, the first generation and second generation . . . find a gap [in] communicating with each other later on. Then, make kind of tragedy in the immigrant family. So we worry about [it]. Their mother tongue is basically a tool for communication in the the immigrant family.

The language barrier is particularly obvious in homes where grandparents are living with the family.

The reason most often given by parents for sending their children to the school is that it would be a shame for them not to know their own heritage. Parents worry that the children will lack a strong sense of identity and pride in their heritage, both of which may create obstacles for them in achieving a successful and fulfilled life. They are also concerned about the maintenance of the family identity: they want the family name to be honored, and they want the children to know their ancestors. Communication between generations is particu-

Korean dance students wait their turn to perform at a Silver Spring, Maryland, nursing home. Behind them are members of the First Korean Baptist Church children's choir. December 1981 (4-29311-26A-27) Photograph by Lucy Long

larly important, and some parents feel that their children are adapting too well to American values and customs. While Koreans do not officially practice ancestor worship, reverence for ancestors is an integral part of the culture.

Most Korean parents demand a lot from their children. Their high expectations stem from several factors. Traditional Korean values stress achievement and place responsibility on children to bring honor and respect to the family name. Children are seen as the hope of the future: the child will take care of the parents in their old age and will continue the family line, insuring that the family name survives.

Administrators at the First Korean School are concerned with both the immediate and long-term welfare of the students and of the Korean-American community. The school offers language classes not only to transmit knowledge of a cultural heritage but also to provide a central place where Korean-American children can be

with others of their background, a place where they can feel comfortable and have a sense of belonging. School administrators hope that the children will maintain the relationships that begin there, strengthening their ties within the Korean-American community.

The administrators are further concerned that the children achieve their long-term educational and professional goals, most of which are set very high. Along with instruction and guidance at the school, they expose the children to successful role models and encourage them to set high goals. As Mr. Han il Lee says:

If you buy a ticket—airplane, bus, train—from here [Washington] to San Francisco, you can get off anywhere along the way. But a ticket to New York, takes you only to New York. In life, [one has] only one chance. If [one has] a big goal, [one] can go far. If have small goals, only go a small distance. So . . . Korean school tries to give students big goals.

*Korean dance students perform the traditional fan dance in a Christmas show at a nursing home in Silver Spring, Maryland, December 1981. (4-29311-2A) Photograph by Lucy Long*

# German-Russian Ethnic Studies at Emmons Central High School, Strasburg, North Dakota

BY TIMOTHY J. KLOBERDANZ

The German-Russians comprise one of the larger ethnic groups in the Great Plains region today. Descended from German colonists who first settled in Russia during the 1760s at the invitation of Czarina Catherine the Great, the German-Russians are particularly numerous in the Dakotas, Nebraska, Kansas, eastern Colorado, and the Canadian prairie provinces.

When they settled in Russia, the German-Russians lived in closely knit, agrarian villages that were established along religious lines of affiliation (i.e., Lutheran, Evangelical Reformed, Roman Catholic, Mennonite, or Hutterite). For more than a century in Russia the German-Russians avoided intensive contact, not only with their Russian and Ukrainian hosts but also with German colonists living in neighboring villages. The major German enclaves in Russia included those of the Volga Germans (*Wolgadeutschen*), established in 1764–67, and the Black Sea Germans (*Schwarzmeerdeutschen*), established in the late 1780s and early 1800s.

The German colonists in Russia enjoyed decades of self-imposed isolation, until the reforms and Russification measures of Czar Alexander II took place in the 1870s. These reforms caused thousands of German-Russian colonist families to emigrate to the New World. Having prospered as grain farmers on the treeless Russian steppes, the German-Russian emigrants were attracted to the plains of North America and to the pampas of South America. The German emigration from Russia began in the mid-1870s and continued until World War I. As in Russia, the German-Russians who came to the New World tended to maintain regional and religious affiliations in their settlement patterns. Thus one finds Volga German Protestants in Nebraska, Volga German Catholics in western Kansas, and Black Sea Germans in the Dakotas.

The town of Strasburg, North Dakota, lies seventy-five miles southeast of Bismarck, the state capital, and about a dozen miles north of the South Dakota line. Ger-

*Sign along Highway 83, outside Strasburg, North Dakota, April 28, 1982. (196618-1-34) Photograph by Timothy J. Kloberdanz*

man-Russian homesteaders established the community in the spring of 1889. They named the struggling pioneer settlement in honor of Strassburg, their home colony in South Russia. With the building of a nearby railroad in 1902, Strasburg gradually grew in size until its inhabitants numbered seven hundred in 1930. Yet, as in other small towns on the northern Great Plains, the paucity of farms and jobs prompted many of the local youth to find employment else-where. The population of Strasburg, North Dakota, at the time of the 1980 census was 623.

Located in the southern half of Emmons County, Strasburg is in an area densely populated by people of German-Russian ancestry. Neighboring communities, such as Hague and Linton, are well-known to North Dakotans as towns where the "German brogue" remains a distinguishing characteristic. While the Strasburg area is

Students examine grave-
stones at the Rosental German-Russian cemetery
north of Strasburg, May 6,
1982. (196613-1-16) Pho-
tograph by Timothy J.
Kloberdanz

primarily German-Russian and Roman Catholic, there is a small settlement of "Hollanders" (who belong to the Dutch Reformed Church) southwest of Strasburg. Large numbers of Protestant German-Russians are found only a few miles to the east, and the Standing Rock Sioux Indian Reservation is located due west, across Lake Oahe and the Missouri River.

As one approaches the prairie community of Strasburg by car, one immediately notices two things: the immense size of its Catholic church, the spire of which can be seen high above the trees and surrounding structures, and the signs off Route 83 that proudly call attention to the fact that Strasburg is the hometown of music maestro Lawrence Welk. Born in a clay-brick pioneer home near Strasburg, Welk grew up practicing an old accordion brought from Russia by his father. Eventually, Lawrence Welk's shy, reserved style, Emmons County "German brogue," and champagne music became well-known trademarks in the entertainment world.

On the northwest edge of Strasburg, well within sight of Saints Peter and Paul Catholic Church, stands Emmons Central High School. The pale brick building is one of two high schools in the small community that are within easy walking distance of each other. Emmons Central is a parochial school that serves the Catholic youth of Emmons County, while the local school district administers Strasburg Public School. The casual observer who attempts to see Strasburg as a homogeneous ethnic community—united by a common religious and cultural heritage—will be hard pressed to explain the existence of two high schools in such close proximity.

The first school in Strasburg was parochial, established in 1910 in the basement of the parish church by Ursuline nuns from Calvarienberg, Germany. In 1918 parishioners built St. Benedict's Catholic School, but there were no high school graduates until 1927. Due to financial problems, the parish turned over administration of St. Benedict's school to the Strasburg School District in 1931. The Catholic parish did not regain control of St. Benedict's school until 1960, the same year in which the Strasburg Public School was established. In 1966 St. Benedict's High School in Strasburg consolidated with St. Anthony's High School in Linton (a neighboring town to the north) and Emmons Central High School resulted. At the time of this consolidation Emmons Central High School was "subsidized by all Catholic parishes in the county and . . .[provided] an opportunity for Catholic education to a student population from seven different parishes."

The consolidation that occurred in 1966 has meant that Emmons Central High School is no longer a community-based parochial institution but a county-based religious school. Nonetheless, all of the students who attend are German-Russian. By comparison, the Strasburg Public School, while it serves many German-Russian students in the Strasburg area, also meets the needs of non-Catholic, non-German-Russian students. The 1982 graduating class at the Strasburg Public High School numbered twenty-five students. Several were of Hollander background (with family names such as Haan, Nieuwsma, and Van Beek). The 1982 graduating class at Emmons Central High School, on the other hand, numbered twenty-nine students, all of whom came from Catholic, German-Russian families (with surnames like Baumstarck, Silbernagel, and Wikenheiser). In light of these facts, it is perhaps not surprising that Emmons Central High School offers German-Russian Ethnic Studies as an integral part of its curriculum.

Mr. Les Kramer, principal of the Emmons Central High School, has been teaching the German-Russian studies class since 1974. Before coming to Strasburg he taught high school in the neighboring prairie town of Hague, where he first offered the German-Russian studies class. Although the high school in Hague was small (the 1982 graduating class numbered only seven students), Mr. Kramer considered it an "ideal school" because of the deep sense of community that existed there. He pointed out that all of the German-Russian students at the Hague High School "traced their heritage back to villages five, six miles from each other in Europe."

The German-Russian studies class at Emmons Central High School follows a general sociology class offered by Mr. Kramer during the first semester. He has designed the sociology course to sensitize students to cultural differences and human diversity. The main text used in the class is James D. Calderwood's *The Developing World: Poverty, Growth and Rising Expectations*. The book is the subject of some controversy with other educators, says Mr. Kramer, since "the United States does not come out of that book smelling like roses." In his mind the sociology class is a prerequisite to delving into German-Russian cultural studies. He often tells his students at the outset of his classes to ask themselves three basic questions:

"Who am I?" "Why am I?" "What do I intend to do about both?" Those are the questions we have to answer, in light of what others are doing around the world. Until you answer those three questions, I tell the kids, life is really not worth much.

There are various areas of inquiry:
1. German-Russian Surnames
2. Map-Making and Study
3. Study of Living Conditions of German Colonists in Russia
4. German Language and Traditional Songs
5. Material Folk Culture
6. Homesteading
7. Discussion of Cultural and Personality Traits of the German-Russians
8. The German-Russian Dinner
9. Field Trip to German-Russian Sites in Emmons County
10. Genealogy and Family History

Each German-Russian studies class is somewhat different in its format and emphasis. And events such as the German-Russian dinner and the field trip are scheduled according to a number of considerations, such as the agricultural cycle and the weather.

A strong, cold wind was blowing across the prairie on the day of the field trip, sending tumbleweeds flying high above some distant rock piles erected by the early German-Russian settlers. While I thought such weather might force Mr. Kramer and his students to postpone the trip, I soon found out that nothing could be further from Mr. Kramer's line of thinking. Following the field trip, as we talked in the welcome warmth of his office back at the high school, Mr. Kramer explained to me that a basic purpose of the field trip was to give the students

a feel for the wind, and the rocks, and the psychological barrier they [the early German-Russian pioneers] ran into when they got here. And on a day like today . . . we can get a feel for that . . .[when] there was nothing out there but prairie, rocks, and wind.

On the day of the German-Russian ethnic dinner, following the meal and program, one of the more talkative and enthusiastic persons proved to be Wendelin Wikenheiser, the eighty-six-year-old grandfather of one of the students. Mr. Wikenheiser was born in southern Russia and emigrated to North Dakota with his parents in 1903, when he was eight years old.

Today he is one of the few surviving Russian-born elders in the Strasburg community. On the day of the German-Russian dinner Mr. Wikenheiser studied the maps and other materials that were on display at the high school with keen interest. Later, he spoke of the German-Russian class at the Catholic high school as being "a pretty good idea." He lamented, however, that the students at the high school were not studying the German language more intensely. He confided that he felt it unfair to have to translate everything into English for his "educated" grandchildren.

Mr. Wikenheiser was ambivalent about formal education, an attitude shared by many other German-Russians of his generation. Mr. Wikenheiser's pride in the success of his old friend Lawrence Welk was evident, and he obviously enjoyed talking about the popular bandleader's early days in Strasburg. As Mr. Wikenheiser was quick to point out, Strasburg's wealthiest and most famous native son "didn't have much education."

*Making German-Russian dishes in the home economics class kitchen at Emmons Central High School, April 28, 1982. (196618-2-12A-13) Photograph by Timothy J. Kloberdanz*

*Model of an "Ulmer Schachtel" (German-Russian emigrant boat) on display in the banquet room for the German-Russian ethnic dinner, April 28, 1982. (196618-2-25A-26) Photograph by Timothy J. Kloberdanz*

One unit covered in the German-Russian studies class deals directly with German-Russian cultural and personality traits. This section of the course always provides a forum for much student discussion about German-Russian values and attitudes. While this subject was interesting, it posed some problems, since the students were unable to see themselves as compared to "outsiders." They admitted that their contacts with people who are not German-Russian were quite limited. Nonetheless, they agreed with most of the German-Russian values and attributes discussed in class: industriousness, a love of the land and of farming, religiosity, conservatism, frugality, and stubbornness. They disagreed with the instructor that German-Russians were "crazy clean," feeling it to be an exaggeration. They did not list other attributes, such as affability, generosity, and sobriety, as characteristic of the German-Russians.

A large circular poster with illustrations of a German-Russian earthen home, windmill, and plow graced the front of the room on the day of the German-Russian dinner at the high school. Two neatly lettered German expressions appeared on the poster: "Arbeit macht das Leben suess" ("Work makes life sweet") and "In Amerika durch Gottes Gnade!" ("In America through the Grace of God!"). A smaller poster, bearing numerous pictures of agricultural scenes, bore the legend: "LANDSLEUTE—Part of our German-Russian Heritage as Farmers."

A characteristic of the German-Russians repeatedly pointed out by Mr. Kramer is an ambivalence toward formal education. He explained this attitude as stemming from a history in which they viewed schools in Russia and later in the United States as threats to their cultural and religious integrity. This fear was compounded by the German-Russian belief that education was not essential for those engaged in agricultural pursuits. According to Mr. Kramer, such attitudes persist and are contributing factors to the unstable financial situation of the Catholic high school in Strasburg today. Mr. Kramer pointed out that many German-Russians tend to be tight-fisted and, consequently, dislike making pledges; but at the same time they want to see Emmons Central—"their school"—remain open. Thus the future of the German-Russian studies class, and indeed that of the very high school which offers it, remains uncertain.

Author's postscript: Rising education costs and declining student enrollment resulted in the closing of Emmons Central High School on May 21, 1985.

# Hupa Indian Language Schools
# Hoopa Valley, California

## BY LEE DAVIS

The lower course of the Trinity River flows northerly through Hoopa Valley in northwest California's Humboldt County. The principal, twelve-mile-square section of the Hoopa Valley Indian Reservation is traversed by canyons and hills surrounding the river valley. The Trinity has been designated a "wild river" by the state of California. Its valley is isolated by mountain ranges on the east and west and by river gorges on the north and south.

The Hoopa Valley Indian Reservation is rich in natural resources. Deer, squirrel, black bear, fox, raccoon, rabbit, and puma are still hunted for food. Among the renowned fish resources in the region are salmon, trout, sturgeon, suckers, and eel. The main food plants used by the Indian people are several varieties of acorns, pine nuts, and lily bulbs, as well as other nuts and berries. The Indian people of northern California also use animal by-products, such as skins, antlers, feathers, bone, and shell, in addition to plant materials used in woodworking and basketry.

The Hupa* are Athapaskan-speaking Indians who continue to occupy a major portion of the territory they occupied before contact with non-Indians. Their territory was set aside as a reservation in 1864, only a generation after white contact. This geographical and cultural continuity and relative lack of disruption (compared to other California Indian groups) are major reasons that continuous language and cultural traditions exist as part of the present-day Native American way of life at Hoopa.

The 1980 U.S. Census shows that more American Indian people live in California than in any other state. The Hoopa Valley Indian Reservation is California's largest reservation, in terms of both territory and population. Approximately 1,000 Hupa tribal members, 800 other Indian people, and 2,200 non-Indians live on the reservation. The Hoopa Valley Business Council, a tribal council for the Hupa people, maintains a Hupa Tribal Roll which lists 1,640 tribal members, of whom 640 live off the reservation.

The educational system at Hoopa began with a reservation school in the 1870s and an Indian boarding school in 1893. The Hoopa boarding school became a day school in 1932. At present the Hoopa Elementary School and the Hoopa High School, both public schools in the Klamath-Trinity School District of Humboldt County, serve the educational needs of the valley residents.

The early philosophy governing the public education of the Indian people at Hoopa was aimed at ending the Indian way of life. About 1880 the military agent at Fort Gaston in command of the reservation devoted his attention to the "assimilation" of the Hupa. Byron Nelson, Hupa historian writes, "If 'persuasion' would not induce the Indians to change, the agents were told to withhold rations, and, if necessary, use 'other means' to 'reach the desired end.'" The boarding school emphasized practical skills. Instruction in manual (or menial) labor (farming, laundry, cooking, and sewing) made up 50 percent of the curriculum.

The learning of English was to be the equalizing mechanism for the achievement of the American melting pot ideal. Alice Pratt, now seventy, recalls the punishments for speaking the Indian language at the boarding school.

We used to get punished for talking Indian at school. I know many times I couldn't come home because I got caught talking Indian. My dad used to bring the horse. He'd come by horseback. He'd come up there, and I'd tell him, "I can't go home." "What's

---

* *Hupa* refers to the tribe and the language; *Hoopa* refers to the valley and its geographical features.

the matter?" I said, "I talked Indian." "Oh, pshaw!" Everything would be "Oh, pshaw" with him. (Alice laughs)

The memory of the educational system's harsh attitude regarding the Hupa language is alive today in anyone who attended the boarding school—that is, anyone over sixty. Many, if not most, of the elders learned that harsh lesson well and would not teach the language to their children, to spare them from criticism and punishment. Forty-one-year-old Elizabeth Marshall says:

When I was growing up, my parents' attitude was not to give us anything from our culture. They were punished at the time. They couldn't talk their language to their people. My grandmother raised me. She said that when she went to school they were punished for talking their language. They had to learn English; and they learned it real fast!

The transmission of Hupa language skills in the home was so throttled by the physical and social sanctions against Native American language and culture that the passing on of language skills within the tribe had effectively come to a standstill in 1970, when the first formal language classes were initiated. Today there are several dozen native speakers of Hupa, all of whom are over sixty years old.

In the early 1970s Tom Parsons began recording the Hupa, Karok, Yurok, and Tolowa Indian languages of northwest California. All the language programs that were developed later had their roots in Tom Parsons's early efforts. The social movement to increase language awareness and skills in a more general atmosphere of an "Indian Renaissance" has sowed the seeds of a hopeful future for the preservation and teaching of the Hupa language.

In the school year of 1981–82, there were five language programs active on the Hoopa Valley Indian Reservation, and a sixth related program at Humboldt State University in Arcata, California, an hour and a half away. The six Hupa Indian language programs are listed below by age group. These are the only classes for the Hupa language that exist anywhere.

Hoopa Valley Preschool

Hupa M'-JE-E-D'N Day Care Center

Hoopa Elementary School

Hoopa Elementary School Extra-Curricular Program

Hoopa Valley Business Council—Adult Career Education Center

Humboldt State University's Bilingual/Bicultural Credential Program

There is a gap between the programs for elementary-age children and adults, since there is currently no Hupa language program available in the Hoopa High School.

*Elder Alice Pratt teaches a Hupa language class at the day-care center, June 16, 1982. (198934-14-14A) Photograph by Lee Davis*

*Hoopa Day Care Center,*
*May 25, 1982.*
*(198493-2-35) Photograph*
*by Lee Davis*

Elmer Jarnaghan, a native speaker, taught a program in the high school until his death in 1980. His daughter Marge Colegrove carried it on until 1981. There is no longer a high school language program and no plans for one in the future. Presumably, high school students could attend the Career Center language classes, which are held at night; but, in fact, there are no high school students in that class.

The day-care center offers a useful example of Hupa language study. The center is a department of the Hoopa Valley Business Council, commonly called the Hupa Tribal Council. It is located in the Neighborhood Facility and is an all-day program serving children from two to seven years of age. This is the only one of the six programs that runs continuously throughout the year—the only language program with summer classes. Alice Pratt teaches Indian language on Wednesday and Thursday at the day-care center from 11:00 A.M. to 12:00 noon. She is driven there in the Headstart van from the preschool, where she teaches just before on the same days.

Upon arriving Alice goes to the kitchen area, where Charlotte Colegrove, the cook, has a cup of coffee for her. They chat and then Alice takes her coffee to the classroom. The class is held in the room where lunch is later served, and it is closed off for the class. Teachers bring in the students in groups of three to six, and each class lasts from ten to twenty minutes. Between one and four classes are held per hour, depending on how many students are in school that day. Sometimes Alice is the only adult in the room, although one of the day-care teachers usually observes the classes. On Thursdays Ruth Bennett will often accompany and assist Alice, bringing specially made puppets of the animals in Indian legends.

Alice follows a standard teaching procedure. She chats with the children as they enter, while sitting at a table shaped like a kidney bean. The children sit in chairs arranged along the outside of the table, facing Alice. She generally starts the class by counting from one to ten, first saying the number in English, then in Indian, while pointing to her fingers. As the children are quite proficient in this exercise, Alice will often have them repeat the counting if their attention wanders or they misbehave. Counting is a familiar guidepost to which

Alice returns the children to focus their attention back to the lesson. She then enumerates the body parts, first in English, then in Hupa, while pointing to the part of the body. Interspersed with this routine Alice interacts with the children in Hupa using such phrases as: "I told you," "Don't bother that," "Sit down," "Don't do that," "I'm leaving," "I'll see you again," "I am talking," "Wait a minute," "Do you understand?" "What is it?" "What are you saying?" "What are you doing?" "I'm glad to see you," "How are you?" "Shut your mouth," "You go, no ears (scolding a child)," "I'll do that today," "Don't say that," "You're scared," "It stinks," and "You crazy Indian, you."

She also will include stories about what life was like when she was a child and about what it was like to live an "Indian" life in the old days: the difficulty of gathering acorns and finding deer to kill, the patience it took to fish, how her father caught a sturgeon in his net, how the old Indian people reprimanded children for interrupting, how the children were punished for talking Indian in boarding school, how strict the boarding school was, and so forth.

Seventy-year-old Alice Pratt is one of several dozen native language speakers in Hoopa. She is a respected elder and a medicine woman in religious ceremonies. Her family came from an area in Hoopa Valley that is just below her present house. Her parents spoke Hupa in the home, and she didn't learn English until she went to the boarding school in Hoopa. She often tells the story of being punished for talking Indian at boarding school. Alice and the other people of her generation learned that it was unacceptable to speak Hupa, that to move forward into the modern world they would have to leave behind their Indian culture. They did not talk Indian to their children, except for words and phrases. Their children grew up speaking English and understanding some Hupa, if their parents still spoke it to each other. As Elsie Ricklefs, the tribal chairman, points out, however, the old people

clung to the language tenaciously, those who did speak it. They thought that it was

very important. And in any matter of real importance, that was the language they'd use, because they could express themselves better. People could understand better, because it was much deeper than some of the translations that we had. People in the outside would take verbatim reports. When it came out translated, it was not really accurate and did not reflect the true feeling and meaning of what the Indian people were trying to say.

Alice stopped speaking Indian to her own children; she thought it was no good. Her son Alex and her daughter Jean do not speak Hupa, but her son Edgar knows some Indian. With the resurgence of interest in their heritage among the Hupa people, Alice has begun to teach the language to her great-grandchildren, whom she looks after, and they learn quickly. In the last few years young people in Alice's family have gone to her often as a resource person for learning the language.

Indian people living at Hoopa are straddling the requirements of two cultures. This engenders an unremitting ambivalence regarding the rewards of belonging to one culture or the other and of fulfilling the obligations owing to two different sets of cultural rules. Many life situations ask for an unconscious decision—which culture to follow?

The children in the language classes do not comprehend the larger context of learning Indian language. Their loyalties are divided. They are loyal to their peer group, which watches cartoons instead of talking to their Hupa grandmothers and plays sports during free time at school instead of attending an extra-curricular language class. They are loyal to their families and are rewarded with encouragement, if the family values tradition, or discouragement, if the family is not interested in tradition. They are obliged to a larger cultural context that is requiring them to learn the skills and attitudes of an active adult in that world. In many situations these loyalties and obligations conflict, and the child must choose over and over which group he or she will

"belong" to. Learning the Indian language has meanings that vary within the contexts of each individual's loyalties, identifications, and cultural affiliations.

Although the language programs were set up to preserve and pass on a traditional part of Indian life, the context of learning has changed and, with it, the meaning that the child finds in learning the Indian language. Traditionally, language was learned in the home, during infancy and childhood, as part of a way of life. Identity-formation was part of the traditional socialization process that occurred in the home and in cultural institutions. Now, since that way of life is gone, learning the language takes place in a decidedly Anglo-American style— in a classroom with a teacher, separated from the mainstream of life for these children. Traditional cultural values have been reinterpreted, capsulized, and then formally taught. This formal teaching creates a selective identity and language becomes an esoteric knowledge. It takes on the aura of sacred knowledge, not the secular knowledge that Indian language used to be and that English now is in their lives. To attend a language class has become a way for a person to assert his Indian-ness, and language is a badge of authenticity. Along with Indian orthodoxy, passing on the language transmits a sense of well-being and worth, which is perhaps as valuable as the acquisition of language competence which no student has yet attained.

Indian language plays a primary cultural role in modern Hoopa because of its mythic quality as a vehicle for defining the boundaries around Indian authenticity. The Hupa leaders are vigorous defenders of their cultural boundaries, fighting against attempts to dispossess them of their land, their culture, their natural resources, their ancestors' remains, their religion, and their language.

If myth is defined as "sacred narrative of how people and the world came to be in their present forms," then Indian language and traditional cultural information are sacred and mythic, bequeathing the story of virtuous and orthodox "Indian ways and days" in an esoteric language reserved as a formal vehicle for transmitting this mythic knowledge. The sacred nature of the knowledge being taught explains the charismatic role of the individual teacher in the Indian language programs, versus the standard role of language teacher that, theoretically, anyone with language training could fill. The life of the traditional elder is the cord that ties past to present, sacred to secular, and thereby transfers the essence of authenticity to the students. The individual is the sacred caretaker of tradition and sacred tradition is what is being transmitted. Caretaker becomes teacher and teacher becomes caretaker. All the teacher/caretakers are women; two men are non-Indian consultants from outside of the community. The friction among the language programs has created difficulties for cooperation and is, to a certain extent, the product of a jealousy over the control of "heritage," over the "correct" forms of the selective knowledge to be passed on, over doctrinal methods of teaching the sacred knowledge, and especially over the "authenticity" of the teacher/caretakers. Alice Pratt is the most revered teacher because she is a native speaker, an elder, and a medicine woman.

The sensitive and eloquent statements by tribal people and community members express the belief that a positive self-image is intimately rooted in self-knowledge through cultural heritage.

The tribe's long-range goal is to get the people to understand the value of their own language. A very great man said once, "If you want to get rid of a people, take away their language." We realize that that's what could happen. We've seen some erosion of our traditional cultural beliefs by our young people. They just don't know about it. They haven't heard about it through our language. So we see that that can happen. The tragedy of taking away a people's language is that finally they are no longer a people.

Elsie Ricklefs

The language program gives the children a self-awareness, allows them to discover who they are, where they fit in their society, to live in harmony with the people there. I think it does a lot for them. They know who they are. They have all their resources here—animals, trees. We're all a part of life and we all fit together. They see how they fit together in the puzzle, so they know who they are. Their singing and dancing [the Hupa religion], these have more meaning to them than it would to me. Because to me that was a no-no thing, you don't do that. Now it's something that you can do because you are an Indian, because you are you. There's more pride in being an Indian now than when I was growing up.

Elizabeth Marshall

# The Islamic School of Seattle, Seattle, Washington

## BY SUSAN DWYER-SHICK

Islamic School of Seattle, June 24, 1982. (198624-1-26) Photograph by Susan Dwyer-Shick

From three families and a handful of unmarried students in the early 1960s, the Muslim community of Seattle has grown to between seven and nine thousand persons in the 1980s. The community experienced its greatest growth, accompanied by a dramatic increase in the number of its school-age children, in the past decade. On February 3, 1980, a small group of Muslim women from the Seattle area met officially for the first time to found a school. Upon incorporation of the Islamic School of Seattle on February 24, 1980, these Muslim parents and educators became the Board of Directors.

The *Parent Handbook,* a twelve-page booklet written by the Muslim administrators and distributed to the school's families, articulates the aims of the Islamic education provided by the school. The school's goals are:

1. To provide our children with an atmosphere, as close to the Islamic ideal as possible, in which they can grow and learn as whole individuals, intellectually, spiritually, and physically.

2. To strengthen them to meet and to effectively deal with the challenges of living in the modern American society.

3. To instill in them a pride in their heritage by enabling them to approach knowledge from a Muslim point of view and by presenting a balanced education with as much emphasis on the Muslim world as on the West.

4. To offer the ultimate in academic excellence so that our children are prepared to take an active and dominant role in the world in which they live.

5. To foster lasting fraternal bonds with their Muslim classmates.

6. To enable them to master the Arabic language so that they may have ready access to the original sources of Islamic knowledge.

The pilot project, a modified Montessori preschool and kindergarten, opened on September 2, 1980. During its first year the Islamic School of Seattle shared facilities with the Islamic Center of Seattle, both occupying a house owned by the Islamic Center in the city's South End at 4919 31st Avenue South. Children between the ages of two-and-a-half and five were recruited by the school's founders. These women telephoned every Muslim family in Seattle with children in that age range, told them about the new school, and urged them to enroll their children. For Ann El-Moslimany, a parent of three teenage children, and the other founders, the approach was straightforward: "We knew all the families in that category." Those contacted responded positively to the solicitations of the school's founders, says Sister Ann, since "mothers of Muslim children know our children need the support of Muslim peers and Muslim education" to keep them from being pulled in two directions.

The success of the school's initial, limited offering provided encouragement and enthusiasm for acquiring an appropriate facility, expanding the existing classes, and extending the program to include the upper grades. During the spring of 1981 the school's founders gave serious consideration to the pros and cons of building a school at a new site or buying an older

building. They finally located a solidly
built, two-story schoolhouse in Seattle's
Central Area. The architecturally impressive structure at 720 25th Avenue, built in
1930, was first occupied by the Hebrew
Academy. In the 1960s the city leased it as a
public education and youth services facility.
During the 1970s, however, it stood empty,
a target for vandals. The building was in
sad disrepair when Seattle Muslims purchased it for $350,000.

"I was in Kuwait when they called me
about finding the building," recalls Sister
Ann.

It was a lot of money, all in cash, and due in
three weeks. I was asked if I thought I could
raise the money. I didn't know, but upon
talking with a family friend who knew
more about these things than I did, it was
agreed that I should try. I telephoned back
the decision. The deposit of $50,000 was
made and we raised what we needed, although it was closer to six weeks by the
time all the money was raised and the pa-
perwork done.

Before opening for the 1981–82 academic year, the school's founders repaired
the lovely red tile roof of their new building, painted and put new flooring in two
classrooms on the first floor, and made all
the changes necessary to comply with city
and state health and safety codes. Although
professional contractors, some of whom
were themselves members of the Muslim
community, completed the major structural
work, volunteers recruited from among
parents, students, and the Muslim community as a whole pitched in on some of the
other tasks. During the 1981–82 school
year yet another group of volunteers reno-
vated a third, larger room for the preschoolers. Repairs and renovations have
continued as funds and resources have become available. In addition, community
members have regularly donated their skills
and materials. For example, artist Jamshid
Kavoussi handpainted verses from the
Qur'an in graceful Arabic script at child's-

*Above: Elementary program teaching assistant Sister Mary Abdi (center) conferring with a volunteer, Sister Jodi Shahabi, about the needs of a reading review group, May 14, 1982. (196610-5-4A) Photograph by Susan Dwyer-Shick*

*Right: A quiet time in the "reading corner" of the preschool classroom, after a visit from the library bookmobile, May 12, 1982. (196610-3-14A) Photograph by Susan Dwyer-Shick*

eye level along the building's main hallway and the name "Islamic School of Seattle" in English and Arabic above the main entrance.

In December 1981 the Washington State Board of Education granted full state approval to the preschool and elementary programs offered by the Islamic School of Seattle, finding that the school met all fire, health, and safety codes and provided qualified teachers for its classes. At the close of the 1981–82 school year nearly fifty children between the ages of two-and-a-half

and twelve were enrolled in the school's three sections: the preschool, the kindergarten-first-grade class, and the second-through-sixth-grade class. The latter two classes constitute the school's elementary program.

Members of the Muslim community throughout the United States and abroad (especially in Kuwait, Qatar, and Saudi Arabia) assisted the Seattle Muslim community with the purchase of the school and have supported its continuing renovation and operation. The Arabic word *zakat,* which literally means "purification," has no precise English equivalent. It is a Muslim's worship of God by means of his or her wealth through an obligatory form of giving to those in need. *Zakat* funds may also be spent in the cause of Allah for the construction of mosques, religious schools, or hospitals and for the salaries of those involved in the propagation or study of Islam whose work keeps them from having time to earn a livelihood.

Besides the payment of the obligatory *zakat,* Islam also urges Muslims to give voluntary charity, to the extent they can afford, to those in need. Indeed, charitableness is among the most stressed tenets in Islam. Since Muslims are supposed to be always responsive to human need and distress, Muslims regard their wealth as a trust from God that is to be used not only for themselves and their families but for other human beings in need as well. The proper Muslim attitude is set out in the Qur'an:

Never will you attain to the highest degree of virtue unless you spend in the cause of Allah out of that which you love; and whatever you spend, Allah surely knows it well. (3:93)
They also ask thee what shall they spend. Tell them: Whatever is spare. (2:220)

Consequently, donations that have been made to the Islamic School of Seattle must be understood not as the largess of wealthy individuals but as an act of worship required of all Muslims in the practice of their faith. For example, Jodi Shahabi, a volunteer at the school, and her husband are students at the University of Washington. They have a small daughter who will attend the preschool in September 1982. Like most student couples raising a family and going to school, they experience financial constraints. Nonetheless, Sister Jodi assumes her responsibility as a Muslim and designates her *zakat* to the Islamic School.

Islam is a complete code of life; Muslims must seek knowledge of the basic tenets of Islam and relate them to all aspects of their individual and social life. In addition, Muslim parents are responsible for the spiritual instruction of their children. The Islamic community has an obligation, therefore, to educate its children in the path of Islam. When the Seattle Muslim community is unable to fulfill this responsibility alone, it is Islamically correct for Seattle Muslims to approach the worldwide Muslim community for assistance. Such an appeal for assistance may have other than monetary aims. Husein Saleh, the Arabic teacher in the elementary school program, is teaching in response to a sense of obligation. "I am not trained in teaching Arabic," he says. "My wife is a linguist and she has helped me prepare many of the materials. My training and interest is in many fields. For example, I have my master's in urban planning. But, it is my obligation to teach Arabic. Each day I ask if they have found another teacher. How can I not teach the students Arabic? It is our language of our religion. It is my duty."

When the 1981–82 school year ended on June 11, 1982, forty-seven children between the ages of two-and-a-half and twelve were enrolled in the three classes: preschool, twenty-three; kindergarten-first grade, ten; and second-through-sixth grade, fourteen. Boys outnumbered girls, but not by much. More than two dozen families were sending their children to the Islamic School of Seattle. These families represented at least six different ethnic or national backgrounds and spoke as many native languages. Some of the families are in the United States only temporarily, planning to return home when a job or degree is finished. For others, America has become

their new home. Perhaps a quarter of the children were from black or Afro-American families. What do these children and their families have in common? The acceptance of Islam, the pride in calling themselves Muslim, and the desire to learn Arabic, the language of their faith.

The preschool curriculum includes Arabic, primarily vocabulary building; pre-reading and pre-mathematics (sometimes using Montessori equipment); physical activity (organized games and free play in the gymnasium or outdoors); and religion (memorization of Qur'anic verses and discussion of Islamic manners or stories of the prophets). Preschoolers regularly participate in the daily requirements of their faith: the teachers instruct, help, and show them through example "to make *wudu*" (wash) in preparation for *salat* (prayer or worship). While the children usually have *salat* in their own classroom, they often also go to the gymnasium to participate in prayer along with the older children, faculty members and staff, women enrolled in the Women's English Program, and Muslim visitors to the school.

The curriculum for the elementary school program includes Arabic reading, writing, and conversation; spelling; religion; Islamic art and music; and social studies from an Islamic viewpoint. Not all of these subjects are taught every day. During the final quarter the second-through-sixth graders traveled to the public library on Tuesday afternoons, studied Islamic art on Wednesday afternoons, and learned about Islamic music on Thursdays. The kindergarten-first grade had a similar schedule: social studies from an Islamic viewpoint Wednesday afternoons, handwriting on Thursday afternoons.

The elementary school children also have regular periods for religious activity. Each school day opens with the recitation of the *Fatiha* (seven verses that must be recited at the beginning of a prayer ritual). Later in the morning teachers devote time to helping children memorize Qur'anic verses through collective and individual recitation. The afternoon instruction includes *wudu* and *salat*, often with one of the older boys serving as the *imam* or leader of the service.

The time scheduled for each subject or group of subjects varies. For example, the daily religion class in the kindergarten-first grade is a half hour, while religion class lasts twenty minutes each day for the second-through-sixth-grade group. *Wudu* and *salat* add another forty minutes to the time set aside in the afternoon for Islamic practices. Generally, the time periods in the elementary school range from thirty to seventy-five minutes. Arabic instruction takes up at least thirty-five minutes of each school day, excluding the time spent on the language as part of the daily religion class, *salat*, *Fatiha*, and *surah* recitation (a *surah* is a chapter, part, or book of the Qur'an). Moreover, during the 1981–82 school year the scheduling of subjects changed to reflect alterations in teaching staff and volunteers, availability of audio-visual materials and equipment, and concerns raised by Muslim parents or board members.

The founders and the administrators of the Islamic School of Seattle have sought to provide an Islamic environment for their community's school-age children, not a school for Muslim children where all of their subjects, except religion, are divorced from their Islamic faith. As Sister Ann explains, "It's not that we are trying to pretend that the non-Islamic world doesn't exist, but we'd also like to show our kids that Islam is everywhere. And to let it [Islam] pervade every aspect of what they are studying." It is this emphasis on an Islamic atmosphere, more than the teaching of unusual or religious subjects, that distinguishes the Islamic School of Seattle. Islamic religion and Arabic classes are part of the curriculum at every level. Formal classes in the Qur'an, Islamic studies, and classical Arabic are required of all students in the elementary school program. During school hours all children participate in *salat*, taking their places among peers and teachers.

Those seeking admission for their children are reminded by the *Parent Handbook* that at the Islamic School of Seattle "education is provided within an Islamic frame-

work, and parents should bear in mind that Islam is not only a part of the curriculum, but it is the essence of the school's being." It is this commitment to Islam as a total way of life that provides the framework for the development of the school's specialized education program designed to meet all the children's needs—physical, emotional, educational, and spiritual.

There are differences of opinion about the importance of specific subject matter and the amount of time spent on different subjects, however. For example, there has been discussion about extending the school day for the older children beginning in 1982–83. Instruction during the day could then be divided equally between the study of Arabic and the study of subjects in English. The school board members anticipate resistance to such a change from the two non-Muslim teachers. "To them, of course, this isn't so important. I mean, they can't see the importance; but it is important, and it's our school," explains Sister Ann. For their part, the non-Muslim teachers fully support the religious premise of the school, finding it compatible with their own deeply held Christian beliefs. The non-Muslim teachers are, nonetheless, concerned about the amount of time allotted to "the basics," the core courses required by the Washington State Department of Education, for which, as certified teachers, they are directly responsible.

Yet, even in teaching these basic subjects, both teachers consciously include religious principles and the presence of Allah in their lessons and in their interaction with the children. During a morning science class, for instance, Mrs. Crum helped her second-through-sixth-grade class understand the earth's rotation on its axis, the planet's movement around the sun, and the relationship of these activities to day, night, and seasonal changes. Using a globe and flashlight she and the children portrayed the seasonal changes and talked about the effects on the children's lives. "When the days are longer, I can play outside more," realized Mubarak. "The time for *salat* changes," recalled Rohymah. Then, bringing an interesting and informative science lesson to a close, Mrs. Crum reminded the children

*Children and teachers in a hay wagon on a field trip to the Aqua Barn and School, May 12, 1982. (196610-1-32A) Photograph by Susan Dwyer-Shick*

that such things are not an accident but "part of Allah's plan."

The children aged seven to twelve in Mrs. Crum's class know why they go to the Islamic School of Seattle: their parents send them. They are also quite certain why their parents want them to go: "Here I am with other Muslims." "At this school I am able to pray." "I can learn Arabic. I can learn to be a good Muslim." "The teachers here are good. They are Muslims, like me." The response to my question, "What classes do you like the most?" was immediate and unanimous—"Arabic!" In our conversations several children suggested other favorites, for example, "Recess!" This response prompted delighted giggles from other classmates who were trying vainly to be serious while being recorded by their now-familiar visitor. This distraction aside, all the children focused upon those subjects unique to their school: studying Arabic, memorizing Qur'anic verses, and working on Islamic art projects. Eager to show me how much Arabic they had learned and to

hear their voices on the tape, many of the children volunteered estimates of the sizes of their Arabic vocabularies.

As to why they like studying Arabic, Lawrence, an eight-year-old boy new to the school, responded: "I like Arabic because Allah made this kind of language." Do they practice Arabic at home? "Yes, it's the language of our religion," several stressed.

All but two of the children now enrolled in the elementary school program had attended one or more schools before coming to the Islamic School of Seattle. Consequently, many of them could offer comparisons of their experiences in those schools with their experiences at the Islamic School. "At this school we learn English," said Ibrahim, a boy who previously attended school in Saudi Arabia. Mubarak, an Afro-American, emphasized that at the Islamic School he knew that he would receive "right lessons." Rohymah, a Cham refugee from Southeast Asia and the oldest girl in the class, observed quietly: "We come to learn to be Muslims."

# Contributors

**Roger Abrahams** is a professor of folklore and folklife at the University of Pennsylvania. Author of a number of books and articles on Afro-American folklore and society, Anglo-American folksong, and folklore theory, he is also the chairman of the Centennial Coordinating Council for the American Folklore Society.

**Erika Brady** is an adjunct professor of folklife and acting director of the Center for Regional History and Cultural Heritage at Southeast Missouri State University, Cape Girardeau, Missouri. She is the recipient of a Herbert E. Kahler Research Fellowship from Eastern National Park and Monument Association to study fur-trapping in the Ozarks. Dr. Brady is associate chaplain at Southeast Missouri Hospital and has been active in clinical pastoral care and hospice programs for the last eight years.

**Vanessa Brown** (Barre Toelken's daughter) was born and raised on the Navajo Reservation near Shonto, Arizona. Later, she married an Ojibwa member of the Roseau Reserve in Manitoba and lived there for several years, participating in and teaching the craft traditions and dancing styles of the Northern Plains. She completed a four-year Sun Dance vow among the Sioux and was given the name Wanbli Ota Wi (Many Eagles Woman) by Frank Fools Crow. She and her four children are avid powwow dancers.

**Beverley A. Cavanagh** is an associate professor of ethnomusicology at Queen's University in Kingston, Ontario. She is a member of the SPINC (Sound-Producing Instruments in Native Communities) Research Group, and her publications on Indian and Inuit music cultures include *Music of the Netsilik Eskimo: A Study of Stability and Change* (1982).

**Michael Sam Cronk** is a research associate with the SPINC (Sound-Producing Instruments in Native Communities) Research Group and adjunct instructor in the music department at Queen's University in Kingston, Ontario. He has worked with musicians at Six Nations, Ontario, Akwesasne, New York, and Allegany, New York.

**Lee Davis** is the director of the California Indian Project at the University of California, Berkeley's Lowie Museum of Anthropology. She coordinates a statewide effort to bring university resources to reservation communities and to arrange for Indian-academic cooperation in California Indian research.

**Susan Adair Dwyer-Shick** is an assistant professor of legal studies in the Legal Studies Program, Department of Political Science, at Pacific Lutheran University, Tacoma, Washington. During the 1987–88 academic year, Dr. Dwyer-Shick was on leave at the Faculty of Law, University of Bielefeld, Federal Republic of Germany, to conduct research on the effect of the German juvenile justice system on non-German juveniles and their families residing in West Germany.

**James Gilreath** is the American history specialist in the Rare Book and Special Collections Division at the Library of Congress. He has written extensively on publishing and the history of the book in America.

**Timothy J. Kloberdanz** is an associate professor of anthropology at North Dakota State University (Fargo). He is the author of many articles on German-Russian, Hutterite, and Native American folklife, is the editor of *The Germans from Russia,* and is working on a comparative study of blacksmiths and midwife-healers of the Great Plains region.

**Lucy Long** is a Ph.D. candidate in folklore at the University of Pennsylvania and a part-time instructor in the Department of Popular Culture at Bowling Green State University. She has written a number of articles on Korean-American food and music.

**James C. McNutt** is director of research and collections at the University of Texas Institute of Texan Cultures at San Antonio, where he oversees publications, exhibits, and public programs on ethnic and cultural groups in the state. He is working on a book about Texas folklorists.

**Franziska von Rosen** is a member of the SPINC (Sound-Producing Instruments in Native Communities) Research Group, based at Queen's University in Kingston, Ontario. She has worked with Native elders, musicians, and instrument builders in Eastern Canada.

**Jeff Todd Titon** is director of the Ph.D. program in ethnomusicology at Brown University. He is working on a full-length study of Reverend C. L. Franklin and the African-American preaching tradition.

**Barre Toelken** is director of the folklore program at Utah State University. He has worked for almost thirty years on the nature and function of Navajo narrative and has acted as educational and cultural consultant for a number of tribes in the western states. Dr. Toelken has helped sponsor student-initiated powwows at the University of Oregon (where he was director of folklore and ethnic studies) and has served as master of ceremonies at a number of urban intertribal powwows.

# Publications of the American Folklife Center

### Blue Ridge Harvest: A Region's Folklife in Photographs

*By Lyntha Scott Eiler, Terry Eiler, and Carl Fleischhauer. 115 pp. (S/N 030-000-0127-3) $6. Available from the Superintendent of Documents, U.S. Government Printing Office, Washington, D.C. 20402. Check or money order payable to the Superintendent of Documents must accompany order.*

A look at the landscape, communities, and religion of the men and women who live along the Blue Ridge Parkway.

### Children of the Heav'nly King: Religious Expression in the Central Blue Ridge

*Edited and annotated by Charles K. Wolfe. Two discs and a 48-page illustrated booklet (AFC L69/70). $14. Available from the Library of Congress, Recording Laboratory, Motion Picture, Broadcasting, and Recorded Sound Division, Washington, D.C. 20540. Checks payable to the Library of Congress must accompany orders.*

### Cranberries

*32 pp. $5. Available from the Library of Congress, American Folklife Center, Washington, D.C. 20540. Check payable to the Library of Congress must accompany order.*

Cranberry recipes collected during the American Folklife Center's 1983 Pinelands Folklife Project in New Jersey, illustrated with full-color photographs.

### Cultural Conservation: The Protection of Cultural Heritage in the United States

*By Ormond Loomis. 123 pp. (S/N 030-000-00148-6) $4.50. Available from the Superintendent of Documents, U.S. Government Printing Office, Washington, D.C. 20402. Check or money order payable to the Superintendent of Documents must accompany order.*

A report on the means of preserving intangible features of the nation's cultural heritage, with an appendix that traces the history of relevant legislation and a bibliography.

### The Federal Cylinder Project: A Guide to Field Cylinder Recordings in Federal Agencies

*Available from the Superintendent of Documents, U.S. Government Printing Office, Washington, D.C. 20402. Check or money order payable to the Superintendent of Documents must accompany order.*

VOLUME I, INTRODUCTION AND INVENTORY, *by Erika Brady, Maria La Vigna, Dorothy Sara Lee, and Thomas Vennum, Jr. 110 pp. (S/N 030-000-00153-2) $8.50*

Introductory essay that describes the project and an indexed listing by collection of more than ten thousand field-recorded wax cylinders for which preservation tape copies exist at the Library of Congress.

VOLUME 2, NORTHEASTERN INDIAN CATALOG, *edited by Judith A. Gray;* SOUTHEASTERN INDIAN CATALOG, *edited by Dorothy Sara Lee, 432 pp. (S/N 030-000-00167-2) $14.*

Sixteen collections from northeastern Indian tribes, including the oldest collection of field recordings (the 1890 Passamaquoddy) and large collections of Chippewa, Menominee, and Winnebago music recordings made by Frances Densmore; and six collections from southeastern Indian tribes, the largest of which is the Densmore Seminole collection.

VOLUME 3, GREAT BASIN/PLATEAU INDIAN CATALOG; NORTHWEST COAST/ARCTIC INDIAN CATALOG, *edited by Judith A. Gray, 304 pp. (S/N 030-000-00189-3) $17.*

Seven collections from the Great Basin and Plateau regions, the largest of which is the Frances Densmore Northern Ute material, and twenty collections from the Northwest Coast, Alaska, and Greenland, the largest of which is Densmore's Makah material. Leo Frachtenberg's Quileute collection represents an early methodical effort to compare versions of individual songs as performed by different singers or by the same singer at different times.

VOLUME 8, EARLY ANTHOLOGIES, *edited by Dorothy Sara Lee, with a foreword by Sue Carole De Vale. 96 pp. (S/N 030-000-154-1) $8.*

Describes Benjamin Ives Gilman's cylinder recordings from the 1893 World's Columbian Exposition and the "Demonstration Collection" edited by Erich Moritz von Hornbostel and issued by the Berlin Phonogramm Archiv shortly after World War I.

### Folklife Annual

*Edited by Alan Jabbour and James Hardin. Available from the Superintendent of Documents, U.S. Government Printing Office, Washington, D.C. 20402. Check or money order payable to the Superintendent of Documents must accompany order.*

*1985. 176 pp. (S/N 030-000-00169-9) $16.*

Articles on the New Jersey Pinelands, the Archive of Folk Culture at the Library of Congress, a lumber camp ballad, cowboy culture, Italian stone carvers, the Watts Towers in Los Angeles, and folk artist Howard Finster.

*1986. 176 pp. (S/N 030-000-00179-6) $19.*

Articles on breakdancing in New York City, filmmaking in Peru, whaling customs on a Caribbean island, the fiftieth anniversary of the *Kalevala* (the Finnish national epic), a logging camp in Minnesota, and the life story.

### One Space, Many Places: Folklife and Land Use in New Jersey's Pinelands National Reserve

*By Mary Hufford. 144 pp. $10. Available from the Library of Congress, American Folklife Center, Washington, D.C. 20540. Check payable to the Library of Congress must accompany order.*

Report to the New Jersey Pinelands Commission for Cultural Conservation in the Pinelands National Reserve, based on the Folklife Center's Pinelands Folklife Project, a field survey of traditional life and values in the nation's first National Reserve, with recommendations for protecting cultural heritage in the region; well-illustrated with black-and-white photographs, drawings, and maps.

### Quilt Collections: A Directory for the United States and Canada

*By Lisa Turner Oshins. 255 pp. $24.95 hardcover; $18.98 softcover. Single copies available from the Library of Congress, American Folklife Center, Washington, D.C. 20540. Check payable to the American Folklife Center must accompany order. Add $2 per order for shipping and handling. Multiple copies available from Acropolis Books, Ltd., 2400 17th Street, N.W., Washington, D.C. 20009.*

A guide to over 25,000 quilts and quilt study resources in 747 public collections. Illustrated in color and black and white.

### Watermelon

*By Ellen Ficklen. 64 pp. $10. Available from the Library of Congress, American Folklife Center, Washington, D.C. 20540. Check payable to the Library of Congress must accompany order.*

History, facts, and lore of the watermelon, along with numerous recipes. Illustrated in color and black and white.

*The following publications are available free of charge from the Library of Congress, American Folklife Center, Washington, D.C. 20540.*

### American Folk Music and Folklore Recordings: A Selected List

An annotated list of recordings selected because they include excellent examples of traditional folk music.

### American Folklife Center

A brochure on the services and activities of the Center.

### Archive of Folk Culture

A brochure on the services and collections of the Archive.

### El Centro Americano de Tradición Popular

The Center's general brochure in Spanish.

### Ethnic Folklife Dissertations from the United States and Canada, 1960–1980: A Selected Annotated Bibliography

*By Catherine Hiebert Kerst. 69 pp.*

Brief abstracts of dissertations that examine the dynamic and complex processes by which ethnic groups maintain their identity in pluralistic societies, and information on obtaining access to these studies.

### Folk Recordings: Selected from the Archive of Folk Culture

Brochure and order form

### Folklife Center News

A quarterly newsletter reporting on the activities and programs of the center.

### Folklife and Fieldwork: A Layman's Introduction to Field Techniques

*By Peter Bartis. 28 pp.*

An introduction to the methods and techniques of fieldwork.

### An Inventory of the Bibliographies and Other Reference and Finding Aids Prepared by the Archive of Folk Culture

Information handout listing research materials at the archive.

### Tradición popular e investigación de campo

A Spanish translation of *Folklife and Fieldwork*.